Essential Life Skills Every Young Person Should Have

© **Copyright 2022 NFT Publishing - All rights reserved.**

This document is geared towards providing exact and reliable information regarding the topic and issue covered. The publication is sold with the idea that the publisher is not required to render accounting, officially permitted or otherwise qualified services. If advice is necessary, legal or professional, a practised individual in the profession should be ordered from a Declaration of Principles which was accepted and approved equally by a Committee of the American Bar Association and a Committee of Publishers and Associations.

In no way is it legal to reproduce, duplicate, or transmit any part of this document in either electronic means or printed format. Recording this publication is strictly prohibited, and any storage of this document is not allowed unless with written permission from the publisher. All rights reserved.

The information provided herein is stated to be truthful and consistent in that any liability, in terms of inattention or otherwise, by any usage or abuse of any policies, processes, or directions contained within is the solitary and utter responsibility of the recipient reader. Under no circumstances will any legal responsibility or blame be held against the publisher for any reparation, damages, or monetary loss due to the information herein, either directly or indirectly.

Want to receive exclusive updates, promotions, and bonus content related to this book and others, plus the chance to win free books? Look no further! Simply scan the QR code above and enter your email address on the landing page to join our email list.

As a member of our email list, you'll receive:

- Insider information and behind-the-scenes insights
- Special promotions and discounts on future purchases

- Early notification of future book releases
- The chance to win free books through our monthly sweepstakes

Don't wait - scan the QR code and join our email list today for your chance to win!

Summary

A person's life skills are the fundamental abilities they've developed via education and/or experience that allow them to deal with the challenges they'll face daily.

All healthy communities and prosperous individuals in the twenty-first century need people with strong 21st-century abilities, such as the capacity to think creatively, and critically, problem-solve, make sound decisions, communicate effectively, and work together effectively.

Life skills are talents that allow individuals to cope successfully with life's demands and obstacles. They are also known as psychosocial skills since they are psychological in character and encompass both cognitive and behavioural processes. Learning life skills is important not just for success in life, but also for our health and well-being. Creativity requires the capacity to grasp an issue as well as reframe it, shift thinking, reinterpret information, and disregard limitations. Fluency is the number of relevant thoughts you can generate, and elaboration is how many ideas you can expand on previous concepts.

Decision-making involves describing an issue, assessing the prerequisites of an effective solution, deciding the decision's aims, and finding alternatives. The human intellect is capable of considerably more complicated problem-solving. Learning life skills not only promotes independence but also promotes the social-emotional learning (SEL) abilities that teenagers need. Experts advocate five fundamental SEL abilities, and we've compiled the greatest life skills that assist cultivate them. Look for self-awareness, social awareness, self-management, responsible decision-making, and relationship-building techniques among the 15 life skills listed here.

You'll need to use life skills if you ever want to achieve success, happiness, excitement, and fulfilment. Skills like critical thinking, communicating effectively, and writing well are all examples. In this course, you will learn the fundamentals of skill development and see instances of several essential abilities. People with strong communication skills are better able to articulate their thoughts, share their struggles, and distribute responsibilities. A company's customer base expands, and communication flows more easily across departments, and employees, all because of the capacity to put thoughts on paper.

Emotional intelligence includes the ability to empathize and control one's own emotions. If you want to be an effective communicator, you need to adjust your message for each new group you address. Get rid of everything at home that isn't helping you achieve your objectives for developing useful life skills. Avoid the TV or move it if it's interfering with your productivity. If you want to become better at something you're currently good at, it helps to take stock of your strengths and limitations in the area.

Individuals should consult their parents about any responsibilities they can help with. Filling out a job application and acing an interview are both skills that teenagers need to have mastered. To better prepare themselves for the responsibilities of a future profession, high school students should get summer or part-time work while they are still in school. The 'boomerang effect' may be mitigated by teaching youth about financial management, budgeting, and creating goals. Teens may improve their quality of life and financial stability with the aid of these skills.

Teachers should consult with parents on the responsibilities that lie inside the homes. Filling out a job application and ace-ing an interview are both skills that teenagers need to have mastered. To better prepare themselves for the responsibilities of a future profession, high school students should get summer or part-time work while they are still in school. The 'boomerang effect' may be mitigated by teaching youth about financial management, budgeting, and creating goals. Teens may improve their quality of life and financial stability with the aid of these skills.

The ability to think fast under pressure is a valuable asset in dangerous circumstances. The ability to control one's emotions is a skill that should be taught in the classroom. A teen's ability to manage their emotions and react appropriately to stress will allow them to take advantage of fresh opportunities and better weather the inevitable disappointments that will inevitably come their way. Being aggressive is not the same thing as assertiveness. Having a voice in the election process is an important adult life skill. An adolescent should grasp the significance of this thoroughly.

Table of Contents

Chapter 01: Basics of Life Skill   12

    Chapter 1.1: Introduction to Life Skills   12

    Chapter 1.2: Different Types of Life Skills 17

    Chapter 1.3: Games That Teach Life Skills 29

    Chapter 1.4: Basic First Aid Skills   35

    Chapter 1.5: Dressing Sense for Teens   40

Chapter 02: Cooking Skills   49

    Chapter 2.1: Life Skills-Cooking   49

    Chapter 2.2: Life Skills Cooking Ideas   52

    Chapter 2.3: Cooking Life Skills Checklist 55

    Chapter 2.4: Pitfalls with Cooking Tasks and Some Tips   66

    Chapter 2.5: Healthy Eating & Nutrition for Teens   69

Chapter 03: Financial Management Skills   74

    Chapter 3.1: Money Skills for Teens   74

Chapter 3.2: Set Realistic Financial Goals 82

Chapter 3.3: Create a Personal Budget   84

Chapter 3.4: Limit Credit Card Expenses 85

Chapter 3.5: Contribute to Savings and Be Consistent   87

Chapter 3.6: Common Money Mistakes to Avoid   89

Chapter 04: Mental & Physical Health Skills 94

Chapter 4.1: Taking Care of Yourself   95

Chapter 4.2: Improving Your Quality of Sleep   98

Chapter 4.3: Managing Your Medical Care 100

Chapter 4.4: Finding Balance and Managing Stress   104

Chapter 4.5: Exercise for Teens   109

Chapter 4.6: Asking for Help   113

Chapter 05: Social & Communication Skills 116

Chapter 5.1: Social Skills and their Importance   116

Chapter 5.2: 10 Valuable Social Skills We Still Need 120

Chapter 5.3: Effective Communication: Improving your Social Skills 124

Chapter 5.4: Social and Communication Skills for Teen 135

Chapter 5.5: Social Skills for Autistic Pre-Teens and Teenagers 141

Chapter 06: Essential Intellectual Skills 147

Chapter 6.1: Critical Thinking Skills 147

Chapter 6.2: Organization Skills 160

Chapter 6.3: Adaptive Skills in Childhood 166

Chapter 6.4: Creative Thinking 172

Chapter 6.5: Decision-Making/Problem-Solving with Teens 176

Chapter 6.6: Communication Skills 182

11

Chapter 01: Basics of Life Skill

Chapter 1.1: Introduction to Life Skills

Have you ever wondered why some individuals succeed while others fail? Have you ever observed that the brightest individuals are seldom in charge? This is because "smarts" are just a tiny percentage of what it takes to live a happy and successful life. We must also acquire life skills, which contain a combination of psychological and behavioural abilities.

Life skills are talents that allow individuals to cope successfully with life's demands and obstacles. They are also known as psychosocial skills since they are psychological in character and encompass both cognitive and behavioural processes. Others describe life skills as behavioural, cognitive, or interpersonal abilities that allow people to excel in different aspects of their lives.

To explain, life skills are often classified into three types:

- **Thinking Skills**: This might include being able to come up with many answers to an issue or creatively developing new ideas.

- **Social Skills:** This might include learning how to form good connections, communicate effectively, and engage successfully with people.
- **Emotional Skills:** This might include feeling at ease in your skin, managing emotions well, and understanding who you are.

The Importance of Life Skills

According to research, acquiring life skills may aid in the reduction of drug, alcohol, and cigarette usage. Aggression and violence may also be reduced. Aside from these larger results, life skills may simply make life simpler. We are happier and healthier when we can properly manage our emotions and form long-term, supportive connections. This is why learning life skills is important not just for success in life, but also for our health and well-being.

Basic Life Skills

Let's go through the essential life skills we discussed before. What precisely do they include, and how do we create them?

Self-awareness

Self-awareness is defined as conscious attention focused on oneself. We may develop self-awareness via contemplation or introspection. We frequently wonder why we are the way we are or why we do the things we do when we have this life talent.

Critical thinking

Reflective thinking that focuses on determining what to believe or do is referred to as critical thinking. It might include arranging information, assessing ideas, and weighing arguments. Overall, possessing this life skill implies that we utilize disciplined thought to make the best decisions we can and then act on those decisions.

Creative thinking

To create new answers, creativity requires the capacity to grasp an issue as well as reframe it, shift thinking, reinterpret information, and disregard current limitations. Fluency, creativity, and elaboration are all required for creative thinking. Fluency is the number of relevant thoughts you can generate. Originally is the number of unusual or uncommon thoughts you generate. Elaboration is the number of additional ideas you can generate to expand on previous concepts. This life skill may also include resistance to closure,' or the ability to have an open mind.

Decision making

Identifying and selecting among options is what decision-making is all about. Our decision-making process is influenced by our values, beliefs, objectives, and so on... This life skill includes duties including describing an issue, assessing the prerequisites of an effective solution, deciding the decision's aims, and finding alternatives.

Problem Solving

Problem-solving is a thought process in which we apply our knowledge, abilities, and understanding to handle an unknown circumstance. However, bear in mind that a problem solution is not the same as an algorithm A issue that can be addressed with a sequence of "IF-THEN" statements (as in an algorithm) does not need the life skill of problem-solving. The human intellect, on the other hand, is capable of considerably more complicated problem-solving.

Effective communication

Communication may be described as the act of revealing, unmasking, or thoroughly describing anything. According to researchers, we may enhance our communication in four ways:

- Use common, everyday words
- Use "you" and other pronouns
- Use the active voice
- And use short sentences

This life skill also entails reaching a goal via communication. We could want to enlighten, convince, or communicate assertively, for example.

Interpersonal relationships

We require a range of social skills to create effective, healthy relationships. These life skills may include sensitivity to nonverbal signs, low fear of rejection, and the capacity to adjust smoothly while going from one social circumstance to the next.

Empathy

Empathy is the capacity to comprehend and share the sentiments of another person. When you are empathic, you put yourself in the shoes of another person, try to view the world through their eyes, and experience the feelings that they experience.

Coping with stress

Another important life skill is our capacity to be resilient in the face of adversity. This might include learning healthy coping skills, using stress management techniques, and practising self-care.

Coping with emotion

Another form of life skill is coping with our emotions, such as enduring suffering and managing emotions. This is extremely crucial for our well-being, but these abilities also have a significant influence on our relationships.

Chapter 1.2: Different Types of Life Skills

Life Skills for Teens

Learning life skills not only promotes independence but also promotes the social-emotional learning (SEL) abilities that teenagers need. Experts advocate five fundamental SEL abilities, and we've compiled the greatest life skills that assist cultivate them! Look for self-awareness, social awareness, self-management, responsible decision-making, and relationship-building techniques among the 15 life skills listed here:

How to do the laundry

Being able to wash laundry is a fundamental skill that promotes self-esteem. Teens learn to take care of themselves, feel good about themselves in front of others, and plan their time for duties. This fundamental life skill teaches kids self-awareness, social awareness, and self-management.

How to shop for groceries

Eating correctly is vital to one's overall health and well-being. Choosing what to eat and how to share it with others requires important abilities such as responsible decision-making, self-awareness, and relationship development.

How to cook

Learning to cook improves self-awareness, decision-making, and connection development. Everyone benefits when teenagers can contribute to the home in unique, autonomous ways.

How to manage money

Early money management instruction allows youngsters to practice decision-making skills and personal responsibility before they have a significant influence on their lives. It's also true that mishandled money causes the most problems in our life. Let's assist kids to avoid that difficulty by teaching them how to manage their money early on.

How to stay organized

With structure, every social-emotional skill improves. The organization has an impact on both you (self-awareness) and the people around you (social awareness).

How to manage time

Teens with good time management may do more in less time. This eventually leads to more free time, which allows people to take advantage of learning opportunities, reduces stress, and improves attention.

How to talk on the phone

Talking over the phone teaches communication and relationship-building skills that need the exchange of information that cannot be seen. This kind of communication is required at numerous points throughout our lives.

How to swim

Learning a new technique to move your body is excellent for increasing self-awareness. Water safety is also beneficial to responsible decision-making. Furthermore, becoming a lifeguard is regarded as one of the finest summer jobs for a teen, but you must first learn to swim.

How to find a job

Teens react quite differently to employment outside the house vs chores or schoolwork. This is an excellent technique to assist your kid in discovering their identity and practising self-management, self-awareness, and relationship-building skills.

How to utilize public transit and read a map

Knowing how to move about without a vehicle in any locale is a genuine sign of freedom. Navigation encourages responsible decision-making, which includes understanding circumstances and problem-solving.

How to be a self-starter

People who encourage themselves are more likely to succeed. The more self-aware an adolescent is, the better the abilities required to become a self-starter they will be. Self-starters are attracted to other self-starters, which may boost relationships and overall success.

How to stand up for yourself

When we educate kids to be assertive, we provide them with skills that they can use in practically every setting. They are better able to articulate their demands (self-management), make friends more easily (relationship development), and are less likely to be bullied. According to research, assertive training may also help reduce anxiety, tension, and depression.

How to cope with failure

The more experience kids have in dealing with failure, the more they learn to pivot and remain adaptable. Failing sharpens their decision-making abilities and increases their self-awareness like nothing else.

How to clean the house

Chores have been proven to benefit teenagers intellectually, emotionally, and professionally, in addition to teaching them practical skills such as how to clean dishes or vacuum.

How to drive safely

It's vital to highlight that being a first-time driver as a teen requires a significant amount of social-emotional development. Teens must learn to deal with peer pressure, make good decisions, and control themselves. This skill's importance in helping youth feel self-sufficient, protected, and empowered cannot be overstated.

Life is difficult enough; let us assist our teenagers to feel confident by giving them the necessary life skills. We're excited to collaborate with The Allstate Foundation to provide you with the resources you need to help teenagers become more resilient.

Life Skills for Young Adults

If you've been an adult for a long time, it might be difficult to recall what life was like before the fundamentals of adulthood were second nature. For parents or those assisting a young person in making the difficult journey to maturity, here are 10 critical topics to concentrate on to aid them on the road to independence.

1. Managing Time

Time management is maybe the most critical skill for young people to acquire as they grow more autonomous. It's easy to slip into the habit of making a calendar for your children and adolescents and enforcing acceptable hours for school, sleep, appointments, and leisure. However, this also implies that most young people must be intentionally taught time management skills to become autonomous.

2. Managing Money

Money may be a tough subject for many individuals to discuss, yet young adults must gain the capacity to manage their finances independently. It is necessary to have a basic grasp of savings and checking accounts, how to read a pay stub and a balance sheet, and how to establish a simple budget.

Credit and interest knowledge are essential for avoiding scams, payday loans, and high-interest credit card debt. All adults must be able to make suitable purchases within their financial capabilities, whether utilizing an envelope approach or sophisticated computer-based systems.

3. Getting from Here to There

Transportation has a significant influence on how we all conduct our lives. Basic automobile maintenance is essential for young individuals who want to drive but lack the necessary skills. Knowledge of how to replace a tire, utilize jumper cables, and when arranging expert maintenance are sometimes overlooked skills that catch some young people off guard.

Working understanding of public transit networks is essential for persons who do not drive (or who can drive but do not have access to one). Fortunately, GPS systems have simplified navigation to the point of just entering a destination, and some (such as Google Maps) provide bus, rail, cycling, and pedestrian instructions in addition to those designed for automobiles. Whatever technique is employed, all adults must know how to go where they want to go and thebe re on time.

4. Communicating with Others

While everyone has their unique communication style, not all types of communication come readily to everyone. Solid phone skills, for example, are required to schedule a doctor's appointment, contact a plumber, or even make a restaurant reservation.

A good job interview is built on the ability to describe one's work and skill set. The global popularity of Toastmasters clubs demonstrates that many individuals, if not most, believe their communication abilities might need a boost.

5. Maintaining Their Environment

Keeping a living area livable is a surprisingly difficult task. Laundry (How much detergent should I use? What is "delicate?" (When should I take out the trash?) What should I throw down the trash disposal?) The labour of keeping a home setting is never finished, from dealing with incoming mail to cleaning.

Even for young individuals who have developed solid habits in this area, maturity brings with it new challenges. What should I do with an extra home key? What is the ideal refrigerator temperature? What should I do if I see weather damage, mould, or pests? It might be difficult at times, but good coaching can help with the move to independent adulthood.

6. Healthcare and Self-Care

While many young people believe they are indestructible, taking care of your physical health is an important component of becoming an autonomous adult. This includes not just arranging and maintaining important medical and dental appointments, but also skills such as food planning and preparation, prescription monitoring and administration, and choosing a sort of exercise that is enjoyable enough to want to do regularly. Self-care also entails learning how to seek help when one's health, whether physical, mental, or social, seems to be deteriorating.

7. Stress Management

Americans are more stressed than ever before, and learning to negotiate that reality is a critical skill for all young individuals pursuing independence. While money, job, relationships, and future possibilities may all induce anxiety, identifying one's triggers and learning how to deal with them is a very individual process.

Some individuals may benefit from breathing exercises or meditation, while others find solace in writing. Exercise, music, and time spent in nature may all be beneficial, as can therapy or medicine. Whatever the answer, learning to manage and healthily deal with stress is an important ability for both new and seasoned people.

8. Building Personal Relationships

Strong social relationships have been related to longevity, yet newly independent individuals may find it difficult to develop and retain friendships after they are no longer in school with their classmates. Learning to seek out like-minded individuals—for example, by joining a book club, volunteer organization, church community, or another specific interest group—isn't something youth should think about deliberately, and it may surprise many people when they approach adulthood.

In an era of digital communication, creating real-world friendships may be especially difficult, which is all the more reason to see making friends as a talent to be honed rather than a "natural" side consequence of just being alive.

9. Setting Healthy Boundaries

Setting suitable limits is closely tied to relationship development. Knowing how and when to say "no" in an appropriate but firm manner to people ranging from a boss to a friend to a romantic partner can be difficult for newly-minted adults who are accustomed to viewing anyone older as an authority figure, but it's critical in establishing both good relationships and a healthy balance between needs, desires, and obligations.

10. Citizenship

Adulthood brings with it a slew of new liberties. It also brings with it a slew of additional duties. Adults must understand how to educate themselves on local, state, and national problems, as well as how to register and vote, what jury duty entails, and how to react to a request to serve. Adults must also know how to advocate for themselves, their communities, and topics that are important to them.

They must understand the fundamentals of the laws that apply to them, as well as the possible penalties if they choose to disregard them. While most of this is addressed in high school, the specifics are often hazy. No parent, teacher, or friend, no matter how well-meaning, can assume civic obligations for another person, but we can all work together to assist young individuals to rise to the occasion for themselves.

Chapter 1.3: Games That Teach Life Skills

Children learn via play, and youth organizations may help them learn by exposing them to a world of fun, educational games that teach them how to get along with others, appreciate other people's differences, and grasp the value of collaboration.

Games developed for certain age groups may also assist youngsters to acquire fundamental life skills they may not already know, or enhance and reinforce abilities they are learning or have just gained. These might range from basic food preparation to gardening to carpentry and sewing.

Blogger Sheri Kruger thinks that it is important to educate children on life skills at any age.   l
she feels it is one of the finest ways to prepare children for life. She says, "Teaching practical life skills and philosophy are crucial components of turning our children into well-rounded and happy individuals."

Kruger believes that every youngster should be able to do everything from meal planning and grocery shopping to two-handed typing and understand the repercussions of drunk driving before leaving the house. They should also be able to replace a vehicle tire, read food labels, and construct entertaining items from scratches such as a rudimentary kite and a basic go-kart.

Junior Games

Younger children are still making sense of the environment and learning the fundamentals of social interaction without parental supervision. Here are some fun activities for kids aged 8 to 11:

1. Nutrition Mission

Many children believe they understand healthy eating, but do they? Ask students to create a healthy eating lunchbox or dinner plate using a variety of foods shown on a poster, whiteboard, or chalkboard. Discuss the benefits and drawbacks of various foods, as well as the major groupings. Did you know, for example, that a can of Coca-Cola has the equivalent of ten sugar cubes, or that the strawberry flavouring used in fast food restaurants to flavour ice cream and shakes includes more than 50 distinct chemicals?

2. Empathy Central

Divide the youngsters into couples, write several scenarios on cards, and allow them ten minutes before acting out the scenario in front of the group. A grandfather who has died, a youngster who has failed an exam, or the parents of a close friend who is divorcing are all examples of situations. One of the most crucial life skills a youngster should acquire is empathy. "Once they have this knowledge and a real desire to heal other people's sorrow," Kruger says, "they will become better people."

3. No Man is an Island

Divide the youngsters into small groups and assign them the responsibility of researching an unknown island. Is it welcoming or unfriendly to them? Should they construct a bridge to get there or a wall to keep themselves safe? Make a list of the advantages and disadvantages, then build the model out of paper or clay, or use junk modelling. Discuss their reasoning afterwards. How do we handle someone about whom we know little - or nothing?

Early Teen Games

Children of this age are through huge physical and emotional changes, and their emotions are often erratic. With these entertaining activities, you can assist the 12-15-year-olds in your youth group to understand more about this period in their life and put at least a few things into perspective.

1. What Makes Me Angry

Everyone gets furious, but understanding what makes you upset – and why – might help. Make a list of 10 things that irritate the youth group members, ranging from tiny irritants like someone trimming their fingernails in class to significant disruptions. Then inquire as to how they respond to the triggers and if their answer is satisfactory. Then, have a discussion. Is it ever a good idea to lash out physically, for example? What about shouting or screaming? In Helping Adolescents Manage Anger, John R. Charlesworth PhD argues, "Anger is a natural human emotion that may motivate individuals to participate in productive deeds or lead to harmful behaviours." "Anger issues often emerge throughout an adolescent's school years."

2. Shhhh!

Children are divided into groups of three and must learn three new and intriguing facts about each other without speaking. They must then tell the group three things they have found - or believe they have discovered. This is an excellent technique to teach both collaboration and the value of body language. We often reveal much more about ourselves to others than we realize...

Kids nowadays are under pressure from a variety of sources, and saying "no" is frequently the best option. How can this be done authoritatively and effectively? Ask the children to provide other circumstances in which they could feel pressured to do something, such as using drugs, drinking alcohol, cheating on an exam, or lying to their parents (this will depend on the nature of your youth group). Then have them play out the proper - and incorrect - ways to say no to peer pressure. Making light of important issues may sometimes be an effective method to get your point across.

Games for Older Members

Members of this age group are about to start an altogether new experience in life. Many are completing school and will be able to support themselves and live freely. These activities for 16 to 18-year-olds will help students consider what is expected of them in the wide, brave world.

1. Getting that Job

Job-hunting has a lexicon that a coddled kid may not understand, so build up a pretend job market in which the best candidate wins. Teens will learn how to explore newspapers and the internet for employment openings, create CVs, and conduct mock interviews. Form an interview panel to determine who is the most compelling candidate - and to assist others in improving their job prospects in the future.

2. Brilliant Budgeting

Make a list of the expenditures that each youth group member believes they would incur if they lived on their own. You'd be shocked how many people believe their only costs are rent and food! Discuss what they'd truly need - food, rent, gas, power, water, incidentals, transportation, and so on. The budget that is the most realistic receives a prize.

3. A Moral Dilemma

Many teenagers have yet to face a true moral quandary in their life and are unclear about how they would behave if the situation arose. With half an hour to prepare, divide into two groups and arrange an argument that will call their ethics and morality into question. "Should parents have control over their kids' sex lives?" and "Is euthanasia ever justified?" are two possible issues. For maximum impact, tailor your questions to your particular youth group.

Chapter 1.4: Basic First Aid Skills
What Should a First-Aid Kit Include?

Put the following items in each of your first-aid kits:

- An up-to-date first-aid manual
- A list of emergency phone numbers

- Sterile gauze pads of different sizes
- Adhesive tape
- Adhesive bandages (band-aids) in several sizes
- An elastic bandage
- A splint
- Antiseptic wipes
- Soap
- Hand sanitiser
- Antiseptic solution (like hydrogen peroxide)
- For cleaning wounds, use sterile water, saline (saltwater), irrigation solution, and a big syringe.
- Tweezers
- Sharp scissors
- Safety pins
- Disposable instant cold packs
- Alcohol wipes or ethyl alcohol
- A thermometer
- tooth preservation kit
- Plastic non-latex gloves (at least 2 pairs)
- A flashlight and extra batteries
- A mouthpiece for administering CPR (you can get one from your local red cross)
- An eye shield
- Eye wash solution

Keep medicines your family might need in your kit, such as:

- Antibiotic ointment
- Hydrocortisone cream (1%)
- Calamine lotion
- acetaminophen and ibuprofen
- An antihistamine (anti-itch medicine), like Benadryl, Zyrtec, Claritin, or store brands
- Extra prescription medicines (if you're travelling)
- Medicine syringes and cups

After you've stocked your first-aid kits:

- Read the first-aid instructions so you know how to utilize the supplies in your kits. (If your children are old enough, go through the important themes with them.) Check to determine whether the handbook is up to date regularly.
- Keep first-aid supplies out of reach of youngsters but readily accessible to adults.
- Regularly inspect the kits. Replace any products that are missing or have expired.
- Assure that babysitters and other caregivers are aware of the location of the kit and how to utilize it.
- Make that the flashlight batteries are in good working order.
- Pack the first-aid kit in your checked baggage if you're travelling. Many of the

goods will not be allowed in carry-on luggage.

First Aid Information for Teens
1. Be prepared.

Make sure your house is well-stocked with necessities. Bandages, gauze, pain relievers, cold medication, lozenges, antibiotic cream, and a digital thermometer are among the items. If your kid is off to college this fall, prepare a first-aid kit for them to bring with them.

2. Know what to do.

Dr Robert Block, past president of the American Academy of Pediatrics, advises kids to attempt these few simple first-aid procedures before consulting a doctor (or you).

For minor cuts or scrapes:

- To stop the bleeding, place a clean towel or bandage over the wound.
- After cleaning the wound with water, use an antibiotic lotion, such as Neosporin.
- Apply a bandage and replace it as soon as it gets wet or filthy.

For minor burns:

- Hold the burnt area under cool (not cold) water for 3-5 minutes before covering it with gauze. Apply no ice or ointment to the burn.

- If a blister appears, do not break it.

- For discomfort, use Advil, Motrin, or Tylenol.

For coughing:

- Use over-the-counter cold remedies.

- Suck lozenges, eat honey, and drink tea.

For a Fever:

- Drink plenty of fluids and wet your body with warm water if your fever is less than 101.5.

3. Know when to seek medical assistance:

- Coughing and shortness of breath that lasts for more than 48 hours

- A cut that is infected, a huge cut, or a burn.

- A fever of more than 101.5 degrees Fahrenheit or a fever that has persisted for more than three days.

- Fever accompanied by vomiting and/or severe diarrhoea.

- A rash that lasts more than 24 hours and burns or covers a big region of skin.

Chapter 1.5: Dressing Sense for Teens

Guys in their twenties may build a strong sense of style by expressing themselves via their clothing. Fashion is the pinnacle of self-expression. Dressing properly is a talent that can be honed with practice.

Remember that you don't always have to attempt to fit in with your classmates. What's popular right now isn't necessarily the greatest option for you. With the correct style guidance, you may become more confident, sociable, beautiful, memorable, and captivating.

Follow these easy adolescent style ideas to suddenly dress more stylishly, look and feel your best, and keep your confidence without breaking the cash.

Even if you are new to fashion style, these amazing handpicked suggestions will make dressing well extremely simple for you to quickly enhance the way you appear with unique and creative clothes.

1. Wear well-fitting clothes

Wear well-fitting garments while dressing as a teen. If you want to look and feel your best, avoid wearing clothing that is too tiny or too large. Instead, let them go to create a way for apparel that fits correctly.

If you want to seem smart and impressive, avoid wearing ill-fitting garments. Otherwise, you risk losing your sense of style and grace. You may also cause harm to the clothing and become uncomfortable.

Avoid wearing oversized shirts, sweatshirts, hoodies, and tank tops. Avoid baggy trousers, which obscure your form and make your physique look bigger than it is.

Also, avoid wearing adolescent clothing that is excessively tight, particularly around your midriff, since they are irritating and unattractive.

2. Accentuate your best traits

Wear the appropriate clothing for your body type to make your greatest features seem proportional and even shine out. To dress nicely as a teen, emphasize your most appealing characteristics.

Wear clothes that fit well, highlight your shoulders, and make you seem powerful, smart, and confident.

One of the best ways to look and feel better is to use your unique features to style yourself. Wear outfits that highlight your greatest qualities to quickly improve your appearance.

3. Wear bright colours

Wearing bright colours is a great way for a young kid to stand out. They can quickly make you stand out, more appealing, and more confident. You'll appear better and dress better if you select the right colour combination for your attire.

Don't wear excessively bright or improper colours for the event. But don't be afraid to use colours. Choose colours that can be combined and matched to make your outfits stand out.

Choose a few bright and colourful things to give a variation to your wardrobe and boost your appearance by giving your ensembles a distinct accent.

4. Choose your fashion style

As an adolescent male, your fashion style influences how you create your attire. Take some time to figure out what you enjoy if you aren't sure what style you like.

Try on a variety of clothing until you find the perfect combination for you. To dress properly and stand out from the crowd, choose a fashion style that flatters you.

Use our extensive selection of different fashion styles as inspiration to help you establish your style and be the best version of yourself without compromise.

5. Showcase your personality

Don't be scared to flaunt your unique personality and attributes by being original, self-assured, and one-of-a-kind. Develop your unique style by using your creativity and expressing yourself.

There are several methods for adolescent boys to dress effectively. You may experiment with your clothing and go outside of your comfort zone.

Wear clothes that are unique, beautiful, and lovely for you and your individuality. They should stand out, appear stylish, and feel special and one-of-a-kind.

Focus on what feels right for you, whether you like modern trends, easy-going, popular items, or wish to deviate from the usual and create new norms.

You will seem and feel much more fashionable if you avoid wearing clothing that makes you uncomfortable. Stay true to yourself and don't try to be someone else.

You may draw inspiration from others, but create current ensembles according to your ideal fashion style, personality, and preferences.

Don't underestimate your ability to look attractive in casual attire. Follow our top fashion hacks to make plain apparel appear stylish.

6. Wear casual clothes

To dress nicely as an adolescent male, choose casual clothing and create breezy looks. Casual clothing will make you look and feel your best, relaxed, and comfortable.

A casual clothing style with sweatpants, hoodies, or sweaters is perfect for dressing better based on your preferences and how you feel. Regardless of societal standards or clothing requirements, the emphasis should be on having fun and living freely.

You may also wear tank tops, flip flops, torn jeans, leather jackets, and any other clothing item you want to seem pleasant, laid-back, and easy-going.

7. Buy quality clothing

If you want to look well as a teen, evaluate the quality of your clothing before purchasing them. Follow our best clothing-buying advice, particularly when purchasing online.

Wearing high-quality clothing is one of the finest ways to improve your appearance. They are not only more durable, but they also look nicer in general. When deciding what apparel to purchase and wear, pay closer attention to details and garment structure.

Purchasing new fashionable apparel is getting quicker, simpler, and less expensive than ever before. Moreover, many fashion firms produce hundreds of current designs each week while paying little regard to quality. Avoid it at all costs and instead, go for high-quality apparel.

8. Simplify your outfits

One of the finest strategies to improve your appearance as an adolescent male is to keep things simple while shopping for new clothing and putting together ensembles. To dress better, get rid of unnecessary frills.

To enhance your fashion sense, keep your clothes basic. Make the most of your closet's most basic and casual pieces.

Simple clothing and styles make you seem smart. You can easily make anything you possess a winner by selecting the appropriate selection of components that complement one another.

9. Choose timeless fashion pieces

Purchase adaptable and timeless clothing and mix it into several attractive ensembles that will stand the test of time.

Classic attire does not go out of style quickly. They are quite adaptable and may be worn for any occasion. They help you save money while also improving your fashion sense.

Simple fashion aesthetics are healthier for the eyes, the environment, and your bank account. Invest in traditional and timeless items that will endure many seasons to many years if you want to look properly as a teen.

10. Stay away from trends

Teen boys often create fashionable ensembles to remain fashionable and enhance their appearance, but this is a horrible idea. Avoid fashionable apparel, as well as extremely inventive cuts, designs, and patterns that are difficult to style and quickly go out of favour.

Cheap, fashionable apparel is frequently of poor quality and does not exude elegance or refinement. If you follow the current fashion trends, you'll rapidly find you have nothing to wear.

Choose garments that you may combine to create beautiful and sophisticated ensembles that you can wear for a long time. Choose elements that are important, high-quality, and attractive while remaining simple and tasteful.

Chapter 02: Cooking Skills

Chapter 2.1: Life Skills-Cooking

Cooking for life does not imply learning to prepare fancy meals. It entails food preparation to live. No adolescent should go to college without the ability to prepare Ramen, macaroni and cheese, cereal, and a peanut butter and jelly sandwich. Add pizza and Taco Bell to their food plan, and you've got a comprehensive adolescent diet!

Any caregiver's objective should be to assist their kid to become self-sufficient enough to live alone or at least care for themselves.

Learning independence and life skills begins at an early age. Toddlers learn how to dress, how to maintain basic cleanliness, and where to place their stuff. Children must acquire higher level life skills when they enter schools, such as washing, cleaning, grooming, and cooking.

These culinary exercises may help certain children who have difficulty with managing utensils due to fine motor, visual motor, or cognitive abilities. This is particularly true when it comes to learning to securely handle a fork and spoon, as well as utilizing utensils to self-feed and chop with a knife and fork.

Life Skills Cooking Activities

Personal Development Cooking exercises not only teach vital food preparation skills but also cover a broad range of topics.

And these are just the beginning. Other significant areas of development that emerge as a result of culinary duties include:

- Measuring objects need math, calculation, and dexterity.
- Scanning, reading, decoding, and processing words while reading a recipe
- Directions include sequencing, working memory, and problem-solving.

- To use utensils, cut with a knife, mix, scrape with a spatula, use tongs, break eggs, distribute an item, or scoop food, fine motor skills are required.
- Pouring from a container, holding an item while cutting with the other hand, keeping a pan steady while stirring or turning products, opening containers, assembling items
- Details, timeliness, frustration tolerance, and organization

The variety of abilities covered during culinary activities is an excellent reason to include them in your therapy sessions when dealing with learners of all levels. While all of your students don't need to be able to create a cake, consider all of the skills it covers!

Sometimes I wonder why I'm teaching a student to make a cake when it's not a fundamental skill. Then I'm reminded of the fundamental abilities required to progress to higher-level culinary tasks.

A student who struggles to follow a simple recipe from a box will struggle to read from a cookbook. Someone who struggles to combine two to three components would struggle to combine seven in a salad.

Chapter 2.2: Life Skills Cooking Ideas

Use these ideas as starter culinary activities for students. The culinary chores mentioned below are excellent starter cooking assignments to aid growth.

- **Cake from a mix-** Simple instructions using a few ingredients. Delicious outcomes!

- **Muffin mix-** Martha White and Jiffy Mix often just need milk and maybe an egg.

- **Macaroni and cheese-** As previously said, this works on a variety of abilities, is delicious, and is a mainstay for children and young people. With some meat and vegetables, your student can enjoy a complete dinner.

- **Cookies-** Begin with the pre-formed ones, or slice and bake

- **Ramen Soup-** What could be easier than heating noodles and water in the microwave or on the stove? Again, it's simple to master, inexpensive, hearty, and tasty, and it can be eaten simply or with additions like meat or vegetables.

- **Pancakes and waffles** are terrific staples that work on a variety of abilities while utilizing a few ingredients. You may scale down the activity by using a mix, or you can use a handmade pancake recipe to provide additional opportunities for measuring and pouring.

- **Sandwich preparation**– Sandwiches are an excellent first item since they require problem-thinking, sequencing, following instructions, and fine motor abilities. This is a safe alternative for students to create on their own since there is no need for a heating element and they may distribute things using the back of a spoon rather than a knife for enhanced safety.

- **Frozen dinners-** Early or lower-level students may need to practice preparing frozen meals in the microwave. While this may seem to be a simple activity, it entails multiple processes, including problem-solving and judgment.

- **Rainbow Smoothie-** This is a great way to incorporate different fruits into your diet while also practising slicing bananas, chopping different textures, pouring liquid, managing blender buttons, and using safety strategies such as placing the lid, using a knife, reaching into a blender, plugging in a kitchen utensil, washing dishes, and so on.

Beyond The Basic Cooking Activities

After your student has mastered a few fundamental abilities, it may be necessary or appropriate to teach these next-level skills. If the learner is unlikely to require these abilities in the future, you might focus on mastery of fundamental food items.

- preparing veggies such as potatoes, carrots, and broccoli

- Grilling meat on a traditional barbecue or a countertop grill. The George Foreman grill is simple to use.

- Making soup or stew in the slow cooker

- Baked goods: baking homemade cookies or cupcakes

- Cooking recipes that need the use of more than one pan. Practising timing noodles and sauce or meat and veggies

Chapter 2.3: Cooking Life Skills Checklist

Cooking skills may be learned from an early age. These culinary exercises enhance cognitive growth, direction-following, decision-making, motor skill practice, and a variety of other skills.

Important things to note:

We've divided these assignments into ages, however, there is a broad range of ages. Some children will not complete the chores specified below, and that is OK! It's a method of determining where and when to work on age-appropriate culinary activities with children.

This list is also not restricted by age. While the ages are mentioned below, the culinary chores may be thought of as a sequential progression depending on cognitive abilities required, safety issues, executive functioning development, and so on. Look at the list as a roadmap for development toward achieving life skills in the field of cooking.

When seen in this light, the culinary life skills checklist below may be utilized to assist life skills development for people of all ages, including teenagers and adults aiming toward more independence with their cooking talents.

Toddler Cooking Skills

These activities may generally be completed from 1-2 years of age, throughout the toddler years.

- Help rinse fruit and veggies
- Pour with assistance
- Tear lettuce and other leafy foods
- Stir with assistance
- Brush butter or olive oil on foods
- Retrieve and sort ingredients in the kitchen
- Sort ingredients
- Turn pages in the recipe book
- Obtain utensils when setting the table
- Help identify items in the grocery store
- Help wipe up safe spills
- Drain small canned foods with a drainer
- Sprinkle seasonings or cheeses
- dipping food into sauces, oils, and so on
- Learn essential safety rules in the kitchen

- Open/close cabinet doors and drawers

More precisely, some age-appropriate culinary abilities include:

2 Years

- Stack cups
- Put the utensils in a basket or caddy (not sorted)
- Wipe up spills with direction and support
- Bring dinner plate to sink
- Cooking involvement that is passive (playing in the kitchen while an adult is cooking)
- Play pretend cooking with toys, a kitchen toy set, and so forth.

Preschool Cooking Skills

Young children gain stronger motor skills, behavioural and emotional management, and cognitive processes throughout the preschool years. These are related to less assistance with some of the preceding chores and increased freedom with others.

Your preschooler may assist you in the kitchen in the following ways:

- Rinse fruit and veggies
- Pour liquids and dry ingredients with assistance
- Tear lettuce and other leafy foods
- Stir with assistance
- Brush butter or olive oil on foods
- Retrieve and sort ingredients in the kitchen
- Sort ingredients
- Obtain utensils when setting the table
- Help identify items in the grocery store
- Find recipes in the recipe book
- Help wipe up safe spills
- Drain small canned foods with a drainer
- Sprinkle seasonings or cheeses
- dipping food into sauces, oils, and so on

- Learn essential safety rules in the kitchen

Try utilizing the following culinary activities to build abilities, divided by age group:

3 Years

- Sort utensils into a caddy
- Help set the table, using support and visual/verbal cues
- Wash hands before a meal
- Help clear the table
- Pretend to play to feed and cook for baby dolls or toys

4 Years

- Set the table
- Dry dishes (non-breakable)
- Pour water from a pitcher into glasses (without filling them).
- Assist with cooking by following one-step procedures such as collecting materials,

pouring, mixing, kneading, and stirring at a counter.

- Cut dough with cookie cutters

5 Years

- Help to make snacks
- Scoop dry ingredients
- Open containers with assistance
- Slice bananas or other soft fruits

Elementary Cooking Skills

Children acquire independence in kitchen activities as they improve their accuracy and dexterity, as well as their ability to read and write. As youngster ages 6-8 assists in the kitchen, these activities may be a wonderful help around the house.

- Cut and dice fruits and vegetables
- Use the toaster
- Crack eggs with some shells
- Preheat the oven

- Use a can opener

- Use a peeler and corer for potatoes and apples

- Spoon and place food items into pans or trays

- Begin stirring food on the burner under supervision.

- Help make the grocery list

- Clean up simple to moderate spills

- Transfer food bowls and plates to the table

- Assist with creating a shopping list and identifying food products at the supermarket while keeping costs in mind.

- Begin reading recipes and following the instructions with assistance.

- Whisk or, if older, use a mixer with supervision.

- Use the microwave with support

- Help load and unload the dishwasher

These culinary duties may be broken down by age as follows:

6 Years

- Empty the dishwasher and put away the dishes
- Pour liquids such as water, milk, or juice without spilling.
- Put away groceries
- Make a simple snack
- Pack a basic lunch
- Make **sensory play recipes** like slime, goop, oobleck, etc.

7 Years

- Mix, stir and cut with a dull knife
- Fill a bowl halfway with cereal and milk.

8 Years

- Load the dishwasher
- Spread peanut butter on the bread

- Read and follow a basic recipe
- Make a grocery list
- Crack an egg

Older Kids Cooking Life Skills

Cooking chores for older children are given below. For the adolescent or young adult who hasn't got much experience in the kitchen, this list is a fantastic place to start. Check out this list for graduates moving off to college or young adults venturing out on their own to guarantee life skill development in the kitchen:

9- 12 Years

- Make scrambled eggs
- Cook hot dogs
- Read and understand nutrition labels
- Prepare a nutritious supper for the family.
- Write down a recipe
- Complete culinary duties within a certain time frame.

- Use a microwave with assistance
- Fruits and vegetables should be cut, sliced, and diced.
- Crack eggs without shells
- Use a can opener, peeler, grater, whisk, and corer
- Drain larger food items
- Follow basic recipes
- Complete baked goods recipes with guidance
- Make sandwiches and salads
- Use the stovetop to complete simple fryings such as grilled cheese and eggs
- Supervise the stirring and sautéing of dishes on the cooktop.
- Assist in the planning and creation of a shopping list
- Clean up advanced spills
- Place some hot meal dishes and plates on the table.

- Assist with identifying food products at the shop and recognizing the cost
- Begin to read recipes and follow the steps with guidance
- If older, use a mixer with guidance
- Use the microwave with guidance
- Load and unload the dishwasher

13 Years and Older

- Slicing raw foods using different knives while maintaining cleanliness standards
- Chopping ingredients using various knives
- Using stove top and oven
- More independence with making recipes
- Using kitchen equipment such as mixers, blenders, grills, woks, graters, and so on.
- Complete operation of the dishwasher
- Frying foods on the stovetop
- Use a peeler, chopper and corer

- Using oven mitts to retrieve hot objects from the stovetop and oven
- Planning a meal, building a grocery list, and shopping with guidance in budget awareness
- Clean up major spills with adequate sanitation.
- The transfer got food bowls to the table
- Reading and completing multi-step recipes

Chapter 2.4: Pitfalls with Cooking Tasks and Some Tips

There will be hurdles along the path, as well as unforeseen twists and turns. Expect them and learn to adjust swiftly if necessary. Here are a few examples:

- What happens if the timer goes off but the item is still not ready?
- The timer has not yet been set, but the thing is definitely on fire.
- Your student uses too much or too little of an ingredient (hopefully they will learn from mistakes or the item will still taste ok)

- There are many things to attend to at the same time, and your student forgets something.

- The thing is a total failure.

- You are aware of certain severe safety issues (learner does not understand how hot something is, or how to handle hot objects)

These are instances from my own experience. I had not considered the variations that occurred in my sessions. I had to relinquish some authority as long as my trainee was safe. There were undoubtedly some blunders and calamities.

True story: For many months, I worked with a sixteen-year-old. One of her primary objectives was to learn how to cook for a living. She struggled with problem-solving. I chose to let her make errors so she learns from them. I reasoned that substituting a cup of salt for sugar, or a cup of oil for a quarter cup, would spoil an item enough to educate her to be more cautious. By some miracle, each of these goods turned out to be OK! They tasted wonderful to her, and she had no idea there had been a mistake. Learning to back up and let go of some control was one of those life Chapters for me.

Cooking Tips

- Start early
- Practice
- Be reasonable (your learner may never want to learn to cook more than Ramen, PBJ and Mac & Cheese)
- Allow for mistakes and issue resolution.
- Change things around so your student may learn to be adaptable.
- Do not be the parent that sends their child to college with no life skills.
- Even the lowest level or tiniest student may often assist with some aspect of the assignment if they are unable to do it alone (I work with a boy whose job is to watch the baby and yell when she wakes up)
- Cooking with students may be both fun and tasty therapeutic session!

Chapter 2.5: Healthy Eating & Nutrition for Teens

Eating properly is an essential element of living a healthy lifestyle and should be taught at an early age. Here are some basic recommendations to help your adolescent eat healthily. Before making any dietary adjustments or putting your adolescent on a diet, talk to their healthcare practitioner about their diet. Discuss the following healthy eating tips with your adolescent to help them stick to a healthy eating plan:

- Eat 3 meals a day, with healthy snacks in between.

- Increase fibre in the diet.

- Decrease the use of salt.

- Drink water. Drinks heavy in sugar, such as soda and sports drinks, should be avoided. Fruit juice has a lot of calories, so restrict your teen's consumption. Whole fruit is always preferable.

- Eat balanced meals.

- Instead of frying, consider baking, broiling, roasting, or grilling for your adolescent.

- Make sure your adolescent monitors (and, if required, reduces) their total sugar consumption.
- As a snack, choose fruits or vegetables.
- Reduce your usage of butter and thick gravies.
- Consume more chicken and fish. Limit your consumption of red meat and go for lean cuts wherever feasible.

Making healthy food choices

The MyPlate emblem is a healthy eating guide for you and your adolescent. MyPlate may assist you and your adolescent in eating a diverse range of meals while promoting the appropriate amount of calories and fat.

The USDA and the United States The Department of Health and Human Services have created the following meal plate to help parents choose foods for their children aged one and above.

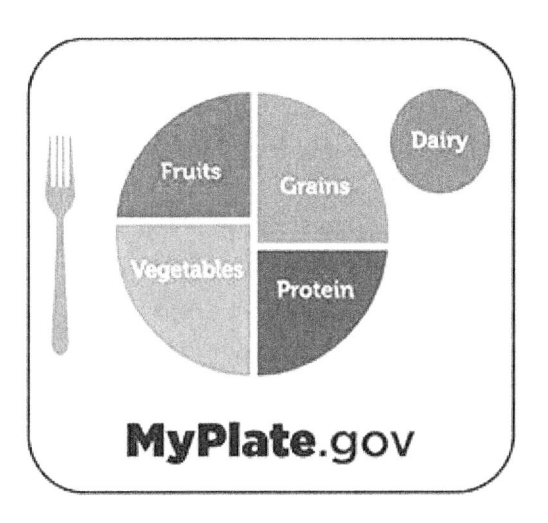

The MyPlate symbol is split into five food group categories, with the nutritional consumption of the following highlighted:

- **Grains.** Grain goods are foods manufactured from wheat, rice, oats, cornmeal, barley, or other cereal grain. Whole wheat bread, brown rice, and oatmeal are a few examples. Make an effort to consume largely whole grains.

- **Vegetables.** Choose veggies that are dark green, red, or orange, as well as legumes (peas and beans) and starchy vegetables.

- **Fruits.** Any fruit or 100% fruit juice qualifies as a member of the fruit category. Fresh, canned, frozen, or dried fruits may be whole, chopped up, or blended. The American Academy of Pediatrics advises that children aged 7 to 18 restrict their daily juice consumption to 8 ounces or 1 cup.
- **Dairy.** This food category includes milk products and several meals prepared from milk. Choose goods that are fat-free or low-fat, as well as those that are rich in calcium.
- **Protein.** Go protein-light. Select lean or low-fat meats and poultry. Change up your protein regimen by eating extra fish, nuts, seeds, peas, and beans.

Oils do not belong to any food category. However, some, such as nut oils, contain vital nutrients and should be used in moderation. Animal fats, for example, are solid and should be avoided.

A healthy nutrition plan should also incorporate exercise and everyday physical activity.

Nutrition and activity tips

- Maintain regular daily eating times that include social engagement. Display good eating habits.

- Involve teenagers in meal selection and preparation, and encourage them to make healthy choices by allowing them to choose items based on their nutritional worth.

- When feasible, choose foods high in calcium, magnesium, potassium, and fibre.

- The majority of Americans need to reduce their calorie intake. Calories do matter when it comes to weight loss. Controlling portion sizes and avoiding highly processed meals helps to reduce calorie consumption while increasing nutritional intake.

- Parents are urged to provide teenagers with suggested serving quantities.

- Parents are recommended to restrict their teen's screen use to no more than two hours each day. Instead, promote activities that need greater mobility.

- Teens need at least 60 minutes of moderate to strenuous physical exercise on most days for optimal health and fitness, as well as maintaining a healthy weight throughout development.

- Encourage youth to consume fluids frequently throughout physical exercise and many glasses of water or other fluid once the physical activity is done to avoid dehydration.

Chapter 03: Financial Management Skills

Chapter 3.1: Money Skills for Teens

When you speak to kids about money, you'll immediately discover that many of them assume they are experts on the subject. As teenagers, they understand that you go to work to get money and that money is needed to pay bills and purchase stuff. Most teenagers understand the importance of conserving money and contributing to organizations and people in need.

If your kid has worked out all of this, they're on the right road when it comes to money management.

We, adults, realize, however, that there is still a lot for kids to learn. The stakes rise as children age and begin to make their own financial and spending choices. That is where we as parents must take our responsibilities seriously. While your kid may believe they know everything, financial literacy is a journey.

1. Needs vs. Wants

Your kid may believe they need the most recent smartphone, video game, or even a vehicle. And be prepared for a well-thought-out justification if you ask why they believe it is necessary.

While your adolescent may have valid reasons to declare something a necessity, be firm and provide examples when clarifying the distinction between needs and desires.

- A smartphone is a need, but the newest smartphone is a want.

- They could miss playing with their buddies online if they don't have a new video game, but it's still a desire, not a necessity.

- It may benefit everyone if your kid can drive to school or a job, but in many circumstances, an additional automobile is desired rather than required.

We don't want to give the message to our children that their desires are unimportant. They may open up savings accounts (sometimes known as "sinking funds") for their desires if they budget for their requirements and have an emergency reserve in case anything unexpected occurs.

2. Spend less than you earn and save aside the difference.

Your adolescent knows negative numbers from math class, so transferring them to money should be simple. You will have a negative account balance if you continually spend more than you earn.

We need to tell our teenagers that if they spend every dime that comes in, they will never get ahead.

Spending less than you earn allows you to pay your bills, avoid credit card debt, save for the things you desire, and even invest for the future.

3. Track Expenses and Start a Budget

Whether your kid works, receives an allowance or has money in an account from gifts, they should keep track of their spending and create a basic budget.

When most teenagers start monitoring all of their expenditures, they are astonished to find where their money goes. Instead of keeping receipts, if your kid has a smartphone, they can utilize a free app like Wally or Every Dollar.

Your kid may construct a basic budget using the same money management applications after they have a better understanding of how much they spend and where they spend it.

Your kid should explore budgeting money for savings, spending, and giving. This encourages teenagers to save money while yet enabling them to spend appropriately. They may give to worthy charities without fear of running out of funds by establishing a donating fund.

4. Save, But Start Investing Early

When your child starts budgeting and strives to increase the difference between earning and spending, he or she will have more money to save.

Consider exposing your kid to high-interest savings accounts to help him or she meet short-term financial objectives. While the interest they receive on modest account balances may be little, educate students on how to compare .01 per cent and 2.0 per cent annual percentage yield (APY) savings accounts.

For example, if you keep $1,000 in a 2.0 per cent APY savings account for a year, you'll earn $20 in interest. A $1,000 savings account with a .01 cent APY will only yield $.10 after a year. Teach your adolescent that you always want your money to grow!

5. Use the Power of Compound Interest

Your kid now knows the importance of using a high-interest savings account. After all, teenagers like money! Why should they settle for a local bank that only pays pennies in interest when an internet bank allows them to make dollars?

It's now time to demonstrate the power of compound interest. When they invest money and it begins to make money, they will continue to earn interest on top of interest. Even if they never add additional money to the original investment, they will observe the "magic" or power of compounding if they leave the money invested for many decades.

6. Understand Gross vs. Net Pay

When your adolescent obtains a job, they'll be counting down the days until they earn their first payment. However, the thrill of being paid may quickly turn to disappointment.

When your kid calculates their salary, they will most likely multiply the hours worked by their hourly rate. However, many children are unaware of or are unaware that, withholdings and deductions are made from their wages.

7. Good vs. Bad Debt

Teens must understand several types of debt. While all obligations must be addressed as part of any budget, one sort of debt might propel you ahead while another can hold you back.

"Good debt" is money borrowed to assist you to achieve your objectives. Student loans might be considered positive debt if they assist your kid in obtaining a degree that leads to employment.

However, the quantity of the good debt that someone takes on might be a serious issue. In 2019, the average student loan debt per individual is more than $30,000.

Before taking out enormous student loans to pay for their education, teenagers should weigh all of their possibilities. Is it possible to attend community college for two years? What about staying at home or finishing college in three years rather than four?

You want them to avoid "bad debt" at all costs. Bad debt often entails high-interest rates and is frequently utilized to acquire desires rather than requirements. Swiping a credit card too often may trap kids in a debt cycle that is difficult to break.

8. Your Credit Score Matters

As they get older, young people may be able to obtain credit cards. Even with tiny lines of credit, your kid might make blunders like late payments, carrying large sums, or simply making minimum payments.

This might hinder people from repaying their debts and harm their credit scores. When credit card debt accumulates, it sets off a chain reaction of financial troubles.

9. Big Loans Can Affect Your Life

When it comes to huge quantities of money for things like vehicles and education, teenagers may be confronted with adult-level judgments. They may be thousands (or tens of thousands) of dollars in debt before they have a consistent job, with no idea how long or difficult it will be to repay the money.

A vehicle may only cost them $10,000, or a few hundred dollars each month. However, young people forget that this is simply one of the costs they will face as they grow increasingly self-sufficient.

When teenagers contemplate college loans, they are thinking about their first "real" job and how much money they will make. Even if they have decent careers, they may not understand they will be paying back debts for decades.

10. You may be an entrepreneur without incurring significant debt.

Some teenagers are natural entrepreneurs with great ideas for little enterprises. They may, however, spend time online attempting to find out how to build their company, including spending too much money to get it started.

You don't want to deflate your child's excitement by simply discussing money. However, you don't want your child (or yourself) to incur too much debt until you're certain they'll remain with the company. It will also be lucrative.

Help your adolescent figure out how to advertise their company, buy the necessary equipment, and locate clients for the least amount of money. This will also allow them to produce money more quickly since they will not have a debt to pay off.

If their firm takes off, they may reinvest their revenues to help it expand. Alternatively, they might look for additional low-cost choices to assist them to expand their firm.

Chapter 3.2: Set Realistic Financial Goals

Finding the proper motivation for your money management journey is the first step. Just make sure your desire is within your financial limits.

More than half of all Americans (52%) are concerned about investing in retirement plans.

Aside from retirement, Americans are saving money to pay off debts (6%), buy houses (4%), invest in education (3%) and plan weddings (2 per cent).

Pericles Rellas works at Abundance & Prosperity as a prosperity coach. He inspires individuals to create lives of power, purpose, and success, which includes managing their financial relationships.

"Before selecting what to do with our money, each of us should assess our set of circumstances," Rellas added.

"The bottom line is to comprehend your current financial situation and prepare for where you want to be in five, ten, or twenty-five years."

It's simpler to make a strategy if you know where your money is going.

Experts advise individuals to start with little victories:

- Pay off credit card debt
- Cut out unnecessary expenses
- Avoid changes to your plan or goals
- Understand your relationship to money

Throughout this journey, keep in mind that focusing on early achievement will make your objective seem more attainable.

Chapter 3.3: Create a Personal Budget

A budget is essential for good money management. Approximately one-tenth of all Americans (9%) do not have a financial plan or budget.

Budgets help individuals keep track of their spending, stay out of debt, and manage their financial objectives.

Aaron Simmons, the creator of the education site TestPrepGenie.com, spent years working out money management. He is pleased with his strategy after much trial and error.

"The most important thing to do to save more money is to eliminate unnecessary spending, stick to a strict budget, and not deprive yourself of too much fun," Simmons added.

A well-defined budget makes spending simple.

To begin, make a list of your costs and keep track of your spending. Budgeters may begin to utilize their systems to their advantage after the tedious work is completed.

Regency Wealth Management's managing partner, Andrew Aran, is a financial services consultant.

"A plan enables you to work toward a goal and track your success," Aran said. "It must be distinct while being adaptable as life unfolds."

Budgets, it should be noted, might fluctuate over time. The first budget you make will not be the one you have for the rest of your life.

Budgeting for the first time requires a commitment to consistency as well as the knowledge that budgets are meant to evolve.

Chapter 3.4: Limit Credit Card Expenses

A single swipe might do more damage than good. In the previous six months, 82 per cent of Americans made transactions using a credit card.

Only 18% have never used a credit card in the recent several months.

The typical American family has over $7,000 in credit card debt, according to WalletHub.

How did Americans end up with so much credit card debt?

Credit card spending is motivated by psychology. Consumers are more willing to use their plastic cards since they aren't spending "real" money. The bill that arrives at the end of the month is on their minds.

According to studies, customers are more inclined to spend more when they charge their purchases, making them the primary source of spending for impulsive purchasers.

To fight your compulsive swiping, consider the following suggestions:

- Set spending alerts
- Limit your monthly spend
- Leverage credit card rewards
- Every month, pay off your credit cards.

If you're careful with your credit card purchases, they may be a valuable tool in your financial path.

Chapter 3.5: Contribute to Savings and Be Consistent

Expert money managers strive to increase wealth and stability via financial security. Americans may attain financial stability by saving and investing money in many ways. According to experts, consumers must contribute to savings accounts, which almost four out of ten Americans (37%) currently do.

Currently, Americans invest their money in a variety of ways, including 401K plans (42%), Traditional or Roth individual retirement accounts (IRAs) (28%), equities (26%), and mutual funds (21 per cent).

Savings accounts, according to experts, are the greatest location to start investing and managing money.

"A savings account is vital because it serves as a safety net for your financial life," said Ashley Agnew, associate director of customer development at Centerpoint Advisors, a wealth management and investing business. "A robust savings account will give you the confidence you need to make better investment decisions."

"A savings account is necessary because it provides a financial safety net."

According to experts, creating a savings account is an important step toward financial independence. It is critical to put money away each month. Taking a modest portion of your income, for example, is a straightforward method to begin started.

"It is the safest, most risk-free strategy to live your life in luxury," said Philip Ash, creator of the painting guidance business Pro Paint Corner.

Ash spent most of his career in finance. Ash's home painting company came to an end after he graduated from college 30 years ago. Years later, he leveraged his money management skills and savings to establish Pro Paint Corner, which allows him to enjoy his love for house remodelling while also providing a respite from all the statistics.

Many employees may attain financial security and stability by saving and pursuing their ambitions.

Overall, regular saving enables individuals to attain their financial objectives.

You must be consistent to put all of your money management abilities to work.

Successful savers adhere to their objectives and only adjust them when life events such as income rises or job changes occur.

Stacey Hyde, a CPA with financial services firm Envision Financial Planning, feels that consistency is the greatest money management method.

"A financial plan is only a guidance," Hyde said. "You're declaring your intentions."

"A financial strategy is nothing more than a road map. "

Hyde recommends updating your financial plan every few years and tracking your progress to evaluate how far you've come.

Money management novices who lack consistency are more likely to revert to previous practices or make financial blunders.

Chapter 3.6: Common Money Mistakes to Avoid
Mistake #1: Delaying on a Financial Plan

Not having a defined financial strategy is a typical error made by Americans.

Financial risks increase when there is no financial strategy in place. People who do not have a financial plan are more likely to be caught off guard by unexpected events.

This might also lead to rash purchasing choices.

"If you don't know where your money is going each month, you're more likely to pile up debt and create worse financial issues for yourself," Rebecca Hunter, CEO of personal finance website The Loaded Pig, said.

"If you don't know where your money is going each month, you're more likely to build up debt and cause yourself more financial troubles."

The first step in overcoming a delayed financial plan is determining where to begin, which requires an examination of your spending patterns.

Different financial planning materials are used by people to establish the best strategy.

Americans of various generations utilize different resources to make financial choices. Baby Boomers (43 per cent) get financial guidance from financial planners, while over 30 per cent of Gen Zers seek financial advice from Google and internet searches.

Younger generations are more inclined to seek financial advice from internet resources and news, but older generations are more likely to invest in a personal relationship with a financial counsellor.

A financial plan is necessary regardless of the financial planning instrument you choose.

Mistake #2: Spending Mindlessly

Using flashy credit cards for every transaction might lead to boredom.

According to studies, customers are more inclined to spend using their credit cards than with cash.

Vanessa Gordon is the publisher of the lifestyle journal East End Taste Magazine.

Gordon has five credit cards, but she sets a goal of spending less than $50 at least three days every week. She, like other Americans, utilizes her credit cards for meals, vacations, personal shopping, and some expenses.

Americans most commonly used their credit cards for food purchases (55 per cent) and online shopping for products such as self-care items and apparel in the previous six months (53 per cent).

The desire to overspend is difficult to resist. Aside from that, credit cards aren't the simplest money to grasp.

How can a person determine how excessive spending affects their credit score if they don't comprehend the fees?

"Many cards will begin with low-to-no interest rates, but will swiftly increase after the promotional period expires," Agnew said." The financial obligation evaporates with a swipe or online input until the next payment cycle when it is easy to ignore or forget." To prevent the tendency for excessive credit card usage, set stringent credit card use restrictions.

"I see our credit card bills regularly," Gordon added. "As long as you have daily control over your expenditures, you'll be confident."

"As long as you have daily control over your expenditures, you'll be confident."

The greatest approach to protect yourself is to only use your credit card for things you need, not for a new pair of sweatpants.

Mistake #3: Letting Payments Pile Up

Allowing bills to build up can only cost you in the long term. However, the coronavirus epidemic has made it increasingly difficult for many to meet their financial obligations.

"A lot of individuals don't have a safety net right now," the National Foundation for Credit Counseling's vice president of communications,

Bruce McClary, told NBC News. "Around 40% of Americans do not have enough money to cover a $400 emergency." "What will they do if they have many weeks of reduced or no work?"

This period of economic instability has exacerbated financial concerns.

As many Americans wait for government assistance, all bills and payments become a priority, resulting in an ever-growing list of costs.

"Developing good money management skills makes life so much easier.," Hyde added. "If you don't have to think about it, you're far more likely to do it." We just have a limited amount of mental energy."

When it comes to deadlines, don't overthink them. Instead, set up recurring payments to relieve some of the stress.

Money management skills enable individuals to prepare for these circumstances, no matter how frightening they may seem.

Chapter 04: Mental & Physical Health Skills

Chapter 4.1: Taking Care of Yourself

Introduction

Your body is a remarkable mechanism. It evolves through time, interacts with the outside world, adapts to diverse conditions, can typically repair itself when damaged or injured (with some assistance), and builds additional machines. However, it, like other machines, requires sufficient fuel (nutrition), relaxation (sleep), and maintenance (exercise) to perform correctly. Without attending to these fundamental demands, the machine will become less efficient and may even break, causing you to get ill. As you become older, near the conclusion of high school, and begin to look forward to a more independent life, it's important to learn how to take care of yourself to keep your health.

Food and nutrition

How long could you go without eating or drinking? In reality, you can only live for a few days without food or water. However, getting the proper water and nourishment is more than simply an issue of life. Because our bodies are so complicated, we need a vast range of fluids and materials to keep us healthy. We utilize carbs as fuel, protein to create new cells and tissue (a continuous process), and fat to store energy. Fluids are required to carry things around in our body (through the bloodstream) and electrolytes are required to enable our neurons and muscles to activate. You thought you were going out to eat!

But there's more: we need the appropriate mix of all of these things. Our brains are normally quite excellent at signalling us when we need fluids or, at times, certain types of meals, but things may fall out of balance. Too much of one item or an inappropriate mix of meals may also create issues. Too much salt may cause high blood pressure in certain individuals, and too much sugar (or fatty meals) can increase the risk of diabetes, heart disease, or obesity.

Sleep

Most equipment needs periodic maintenance and cooling down. Your brain is most likely the most intricate organ of your body, yet we are just now starting to comprehend how it works. But one thing is certain: our brain and body need sleep to function correctly in terms of thinking, memory, attention, and decision-making.

Nobody understands precisely how sleep occurs, but we do know that when sleeping, we take in less information from the outside world and organize information in our brains. And we can't go long without sleep before our performance drops significantly. Have you ever remained up for the whole 24 hours? What were your thoughts? People who are sleep deprived often struggle with even the most basic tasks, such as writing or driving.

Young people normally need at least 8 hours of sleep every night to feel and operate well – and may require more. The good news is that if you don't get enough sleep one night, you can generally make up for it the following night by having a decent night's sleep.

Exercise

Just as your body needs rest to restore itself, it also requires frequent usage to function well - and the way we utilize our bodies is through moving. When you think about it, exercise is just moving in a systematic (and often repeated) manner. However, using our bodies in this manner benefits almost every portion of our bodies. Exercise, of course, stimulates our muscles, but it also works our hearts and lungs over time (this is generally referred to as "cardio" or aerobic training). Many activities help strengthen our bones, and there is even evidence that exercise improves the efficiency of our brains!

You can join a gym or run a marathon to benefit from fitness. Walking to school, playing ball, mowing the yard, going on a hike, and washing dishes or laundry are all examples of regular activities that provide exercise. The idea is to train as many various portions of your body as possible regularly and to move for 20-30 minutes several times each week. You do not need to overdo it - and it is possible to overdo it (among other things you can injure yourself, get overheated, dehydrated, and damage muscles for overexercising). However, it is essential and beneficial to keep your body active!

Chapter 4.2: Improving Your Quality of Sleep

The amount of sleep is crucial, but so is the quality. The quality of your sleep each night has a significant influence on your health and functioning, so if you believe your sleep hygiene may be improved, keep reading for suggestions.

- **A cool, dark and quiet room = good sleep.** Begin your journey to enhance your sleep quality by taking a glance at yourself. Consider purchasing a fan, a white noise machine, and/or black-out curtains if you don't already have them to make your area more attractive for a good night's sleep.

- **Avoid gaming, Tweeting, Netflix Ing and posting in bed.** It's OK to do these things to relax after a hard day, but make sure you don't do them in bed. Electronics should ideally be avoided at least an hour before bedtime to avoid interfering with your body's synthesis of the sleep-inducing hormone melatonin. Blue light from computer displays, smartphones, and TVs halts its production, causing you to toss and turn (and cranky in the morning).

- **Eat well and exercise.** It should come as no surprise that your food and exercise routine might have an impact on the quality of your sleep. If you want to maximize your snoozing, make sure the rest of your life is in order. Avoid strenuous exertion soon before bedtime. This stimulates your heart, brain, and muscles, which is the opposite of what you want before going to bed.

- **Avoid caffeine, nicotine and alcohol.** All three have an impact on the quality of your sleep. Avoiding them, especially in the afternoon and evening, may help you get more sleep.

- **Develop a sleep routine.** Try to do the same activity every night 30 minutes to an hour before bed, such as reading, taking a bath, or writing in your notebook about your day. You can teach your brain to recognize when it's time to sleep over time. Setting precise times to go to bed and wake up each day might also assist to enhance your sleep quality by controlling your internal clock.

- **Experiment**. Everyone's sleep demands vary, so try out various strategies, keep note of how well you sleep under different settings and figure out what works best for you.

Chapter 4.3: Managing Your Medical Care
The High School Years

You've probably spent most of your life attending to a family doctor or a paediatrician. You've had at least one annual check-up, vaccinations if you're travelling or beginning a new school or camp, and if you're ill, you've notified a parent and one of you has phoned the doctor to schedule an appointment (probably more often than not, a parent).

This procedure will shift significantly as you grow older and develop more freedom. Whether or not you go to college after high school, you will most likely need to transition from seeing a paediatrician, a doctor for children, to seeing an adult healthcare practitioner.

Before you attempt to locate a new medical provider, do the following steps: Instead of having a parent or guardian schedule an appointment for you, make one with your present doctor. Discuss your medical history with your parents: you'll need to know your own and your family's medical histories since they'll likely come upon medical paperwork when you visit with a new doctor. It is also crucial to talk to your family about your existing health insurance and how it will continue or change when you go to college.

Before you can make any appointments, you must first compile a list of certified specialists (and whether they work with your insurance plan). If you want to live at or near home, your paediatrician will almost certainly be able to suggest a doctor in his or her network. Your parents or siblings may also give suggestions. Look at where these physicians work:

is it close to your home or place of residence? Is the office accessible to people with disabilities?

There are many things to ask while looking for a new doctor to address both physical and mental health concerns. Setting up a meeting with prospective physicians before agreeing to become their patient might help you answer these questions.

Having an adult healthcare provider may help you maintain your independence. You must be open and honest about your activities, background, and worries, as well as pay attention to how you feel, both physically and emotionally, and take necessary action to get yourself treatment. This may seem difficult, but everyone can learn to do it, and it will assist you on your way to being an independent, self-sufficient adult.

Leading Up to Graduation

Several health difficulties will arise after you graduate from high school. You will need the services of an adult doctor rather than a paediatrician. Your new doctor will be better equipped to help you with the specific issues that come with becoming an adult. Consider which kind of physicians you will need: will you simply require a primary care physician? Will you need the services of a psychiatrist? Request that your paediatrician recommends physicians in your area, and make one or more visits with these doctors.

If you relocate, you will need to find and schedule visits with whole new physicians. Check to see whether you like these physicians - fit is key when looking for a new provider, particularly if he or she provides mental health care. Before booking appointments, consider your preferred approach.

You will also need to consider your insurance options: you may continue to use your parents' insurance, enrol in a plan supplied by your institution, or enrol in a plan offered by an employer. Regardless, get acquainted with your insurance plan and the locations where it is accepted. Meeting with a doctor to evaluate whether he or she is a good match is unlikely to be covered by your insurance.

Whether you relocate, remain at home, and look for a job right away, or go to college after high school, you will have to adapt to dealing with your own physical and emotional health. It is very beneficial to have proper assistance when you enter adulthood to be self-sufficient and healthy, both physically and emotionally.

Remember that as you gain independence and take more responsibility for your care, your family and prior physicians and healthcare professionals are still there to give advice and support as required.

Chapter 4.4: Finding Balance and Managing Stress

Erik Erikson, a psychologist, stated that the three major aims or activities in life were to love (including friendships, family, and romantic connections), work (including school), and play (having fun and being creative). Working on balancing these three fundamental life factors as you travel through life can help put you on the route to a full, meaningful, and balanced existence.

As we get older, we should learn to connect with, relate to, and love people. We also learn how to study, manage our duties, and stay to and finish assignments (work). And, if we're fortunate, we learn to explore the world, play games, and have fun.

And, while we learn to love, work, and play, we must also be able to discern how to maintain ourselves balanced, adaptable, and focused. There are periods in life when the balance has to be more on schooling (getting ready for examinations, for example), and other times when you may put more energy into play (trying to make a sports team, for example) or love (your friend is having trouble and needs help). Being conscious of the need for flexibility and modifications assists us in maintaining our fundamental life balance.

The pursuit of balance is an ongoing endeavour, but if you start thinking about these fundamental concepts now and keep them in mind throughout your life, you'll be off to a wonderful start!

Life is full of stressful situations. That is why it is important to learn how to handle stress now so that you are prepared to cope with it later in life, particularly once you graduate from high school and become more self-sufficient. A certain degree of stress may be good and motivating; but, when this level is exceeded, stress can become a problem. When stress becomes too great to bear, it may hurt your health, job and school performance, and social life. This is because stress may influence your mood and even your capacity to think rationally. Stress may also impair your immune system, making you more prone to illness. Health problems such as high blood pressure, autoimmune illness, digestive disorders, depression, and anxiety may occasionally develop and/or worsen if left untreated (i.e., chronic stress).

Fortunately, there are several methods for managing stress and keeping it at a healthy level. The idea is to create a lifestyle that integrates stress-reduction activities and tactics; learn to identify the causes and indicators of stress, and be proactive in managing stress when it becomes too severe. Continue reading for stress-reduction techniques!

Sleep, nutrition and exercise

You may have realized by now that physical and mental wellness are inextricably linked. Maintaining your physical health benefits your mental health - and vice versa!

Getting adequate sleep, eating a good diet, and scheduling regular exercise are all well-known stress relievers.

Know your stress triggers and signs of stress overload

To battle stress and keep it from becoming a problem, you must first understand your stress triggers and indicators of stress overload. Consider times when you were anxious. Did you have any persons, locations, or circumstances in common? These are your stressors. If you know you'll be around certain people, locations, or circumstances, prepare for them ahead of time to reduce stress.

Memory issues, difficulty focusing, irritability, headaches, recurrent colds, and changes in sleep or appetite are all classic symptoms of stress overload. If you experience any of these symptoms, you may be too stressed and should adopt some of the other suggestions in these cards into your life.

Try relaxation techniques

When you are agitated, your fight-or-flight reaction activates, releasing multiple hormones throughout your body that, among other things, increase your heart rate and breathing rate while slowing your digestion. Repetition of this reaction fatigues the body and may result in undesirable consequences such as difficulty focusing and a compromised immune system. While it is impossible (and harmful) to remove all stress from your life, you can influence how you respond to stress, and relaxing methods may assist. Yoga, breathing exercises, meditation, and visualization are all techniques that may help you relax. To get the most advantages, try to arrange a 10-minute relaxation break every day.

Be smart with your time

There are various methods for efficiently managing your time to reduce stress. First, make a note of everything you need to accomplish in your planner or phone, then prioritize your list and divide tasks into single stages or activities. Additionally, concentrate on one activity at a time - multitasking seldom works. Finally, and most importantly, be realistic with your time and try not to over-commit yourself - although it may be easy to say yes to everything, pulling yourself in several ways is stressful and simply adds to your stress.

Curb your caffeine

Caffeine may seem to help you study or work on that project for longer periods by offering an energy boost, but research indicates that even if you are more aware, you are just as likely to make mistakes on coffee or caffeinated beverages as you would if you did not consume them. Caffeine, especially if you are already worried, may make you feel even more anxious, tight, and jittery, which increases your stress level. Drink no more than one caffeinated beverage per day, and avoid it in the afternoon and evening since it might disrupt your sleep cycle and prevent you from obtaining a decent night's sleep, which we all know is essential for stress management.

Reach out

If you're feeling too worried, speak to a friend or family member about it. They may have been in a scenario similar to yours that is causing you stress and may be able to provide helpful insight and guidance to assist you to lessen your stress. It's also a good idea to go to a counsellor or therapist if your stress is out of control despite your best efforts to reduce it. Therapists may help you discover and understand the underlying causes of your stress, as well as lead you through some of the previously outlined beneficial relaxation strategies.

Because everyone feels stress differently, the best techniques to handle stress vary as well. Take the time to try out any or all of the options above to see what works best for you.

Chapter 4.5: Exercise for Teens

Teens must exercise to stay healthy. Encouraging healthy habits in children and teenagers is critical for their future success. Childhood lifestyle choices are more likely to be carried over into adulthood. Some lifestyle modifications may be more difficult to implement as a person matures. The greatest method to encourage healthy habits is to include the whole family.

Establishing An Exercise Plan

A daily exercise program is a pleasant approach to enjoying physical activity with family and friends while establishing healthy cardiac behaviours. The following adolescent fitness suggestions might assist you and your teen in planning activities:

- Teenagers need at least 60 minutes of moderate to strenuous physical exercise on most days to maintain excellent health and fitness and to maintain a healthy weight throughout growing.

- Parents are recommended to restrict their teen's screen time (TV, video games, and computers) to less than 2 hours per day and to replace these sitting activities with more active ones.

Even 30 minutes of low-to-moderate intensity activity each day might be beneficial. Among these activities are the following:

- Pleasure walking
- Climbing stairs
- Dancing
- Home exercise

A teen's capacity for exercise grows with regular aerobic physical activity. It also aids in the prevention of cardiovascular disease and type 2 diabetes. Aerobic activities are ongoing activities that raise the heart rate and breathing rate. Encourage your adolescent to consume fluids often during physical activities to avoid dehydration. Also, following the physical exercise, have them drink several glasses of water or another non-sugary beverage. Examples of strenuous exercises include:

- Brisk walking
- Running
- Swimming
- Cycling
- Roller skating
- Jumping rope
- Playing on the playground
- Dancing
- Gymnastics
- Hiking
- Soccer
- Tag games

Daily exercise may help avoid obesity, high blood pressure, and abnormal cholesterol levels in teenagers, as well as bad lifestyle patterns that contribute to heart attack and stroke later in life.

Regular exercise is an important aspect of living a healthy lifestyle. However, some teens may over-exercise. If your adolescent starts to lose weight and falls short of typical development trends, or if exercise interferes with other routine activities, such as school, you should consult with your teen's healthcare professional.

Benefits From Regular Exercise or Physical Activity

The following are important advantages of physical exercise, according to the American Heart Association and the President's Council on Fitness, Sports, and Nutrition:

- Improves blood circulation throughout the body
- Keeps weight under control
- Improves blood cholesterol levels
- Prevents and manages high blood pressure
- Prevents bone loss

- Boosts energy level
- Releases tension
- Improves the ability to fall asleep quickly and sleep well
- Improves self-image
- Helps manage stress
- Fights anxiety and depression
- Increases enthusiasm and optimism
- Increases muscle strength

Chapter 4.6: Asking for Help

One of the most significant changes we go through as we get older is being more competent and self-sufficient. We grow better at doing things on our own. However, as we gain independence and self-sufficiency, we must learn when to handle or solve problems on our own and when to seek assistance from others.

It is a question of striking the right balance when it comes to asking for aid. On the one hand, when presented with a problem, there is undeniable benefit in attempting to master it oneself. Consider doing something like assembling a puzzle or solving a math problem. If you can figure things out on your own with some time and effort, you will most likely learn more and feel more accomplished. But suppose the puzzle involves millions of pieces or you were absent from school on the day the math subject was presented and you need to complete the problem for homework. So, what now?

Here are some questions to consider when deciding whether to seek assistance:

- Is there any way I can figure this out/solve the problem/face the challenge on my own? Let's return to the math issue. It makes sense to do it yourself if you have most of what you need to try figuring it out, understand what you're lacking, and have a decent probability of finding the information in your book or online.

- Can you start thinking about a solution to the problem? Assume you had an argument with a buddy, and you've had comparable conflicts with another friend and were able to resolve them. It could be appropriate to repeat what you did this time.

- Is this a difficulty or issue that you can manage on your own? If your parent asks you to move anything in the home that isn't very heavy, you should be able to accomplish it. If they ask you to lift anything weighing 100 pounds, you will almost certainly need the assistance of a buddy (or two).

- How much time do you have to address the problem? Even if you think you can do it yourself, if it will take too long or has to be done right immediately, hiring assistance makes sense.

You've undoubtedly noticed that we make decisions about when to seek assistance all the time without even thinking about it. However, if you study how you make these judgments when they arise, you will see that most of us follow basic common sense rules.

When you are unsure, consider these questions to help you determine if it is appropriate to seek assistance. Remember that as you become older and more autonomous, your life will get more complicated - frequently in a good way! However, the intricacy compels us to recognize when it is desirable and acceptable to seek support or assistance. It's great to be able to depend on yourself to get things done, but it also makes sense to ask for assistance from time to time - try to strike a balance that works for you!

Chapter 05: Social & Communication Skills

Chapter 5.1: Social Skills and their Importance

Social skills are necessary for establishing personal and professional interactions. Strong interpersonal skills assist you in achieving your objectives, contributing to corporate successes, performing effectively during the recruiting process, and expanding your professional network. Understanding and strengthening your social skills may help you in many aspects of your life.

Social Skills

Social skills are utilized every day to interact with people in several ways, including spoken, nonverbal, written, and visual communication. Social skills are often known as "interpersonal skills" or "soft talents."

Nonverbal communication comprises body language, facial expressions, and eye contact, while verbal communication includes spoken words. You use social skills every time you engage with another individual. Strong social skills may help you create and maintain effective professional and personal connections.

Why Social Skills Are Important

Social skills are crucial because they allow you to communicate more effectively and efficiently, allowing you to develop, maintain, and strengthen connections with coworkers, customers, and new contacts. These abilities are critical to keep and grow regardless of your job, sector, or degree of experience.

There are several benefits to having strong social skills.

Here are five examples:

1. More and Better Relationships

Identification with others leads to greater interactions and, at times, friendships.

By improving your social abilities, you will become more charismatic, which is a desired characteristic. Individuals are more interested in charismatic people because charismatic people seem to be more interested in them.

Most individuals understand that you cannot grow in life unless you have good interpersonal interactions. Concentrating on relationships can help you acquire a job, advance in your career, and establish new friends. Well-honed social skills may boost your happiness and contentment while also improving your view on life.

More connections may also aid in reducing the negative impacts of stress and boosting your self-esteem.

2. Better Communication

Being able to relate to people and work in big groups automatically improves one's communication abilities.

After all, you can't have excellent social skills unless you have solid communication abilities, and being able to articulate one's thoughts and ideas may be the most crucial talent you can learn in life.

3. Greater Efficiency

If you are excellent with people, you may avoid spending time with individuals you don't like as much as others.

Some people dislike social contacts because they do not want to spend time with people who do not share their interests and perspectives. Attending a meeting at work or a party in your personal life is much simpler if you know at least some of the individuals who will be there.

If you are in a social scenario and do not want to spend time with 'John' because you dislike him or he cannot assist you with a specific problem, a decent set of social skills will enable you to respectfully indicate that you need to spend time with other individuals at the gathering.

See our sites on increasing self-esteem and confidence.

4. Advancing Career Prospects

Most good occupations include a "people component," and the most profitable roles often need extensive interaction with workers, the media, and colleagues.

It is unusual for someone to be secluded at their workplace and yet flourish in their profession. Most firms want employees with a specific, tactical skill set: the ability to work effectively in a team and to influence and encourage others to get things done.

For additional information on the kind of skills that companies need, see our pages on Employability Skills and Transferable Skills.

5. Increased Overall Happiness

Understanding and getting along with others can help you open numerous personal and professional doors.

Being able to strike up a discussion at a work-related conference may result in a new job offer with a better income. In a social context, a grin and a "hello" might lead to the formation of a friendship.

Chapter 5.2: 10 Valuable Social Skills We Still Need

With social media consuming so much of our free (and not-so-free) time, what we formerly considered crucial and useful social skills seem to be fading. Do we even need them?

We certainly do - now more than ever!

We still need to know how to engage effectively with coworkers, managers, customers, friends, and others we meet regularly. Simply stated, we must learn how to get along with others.

Another term for social skills is social intelligence,' which was originally examined and investigated by psychologist Edward Thorndike in 1920. He described it as the capacity to engage with people successfully in every social circumstance, or "to behave intelligently in human interactions."

Here are some useful social skills:

1. **Effective communication.** You must learn how to communicate effectively to successfully express your thoughts, views, and ideas to others. We may rapidly convert a message into a mistake, generate confusion, or create a tragedy if we lack the skill to communicate clearly and effectively.
2. **Active listening.** Listening is a social ability that is undervalued. To participate in good communication, you must know and comprehend what the other person is saying, which can only be accomplished through actively listening. Listening actively is paying attention to and absorbing what the

other person is saying rather than planning your next words.

3. **Making eye contact.** Making eye contact with someone while they are speaking is one technique to convey that you are paying attention to what they are saying. When seeking to connect with someone, gazing at your phone or elsewhere is NOT appropriate. Making eye contact indicates that you are paying attention.

4. **Learning people's names.** Nothing validates you more than when someone recalls and uses your name after you've just been introduced, or whether you're an acquaintance, friendly grocer, or cashier. We all want to feel important, and hearing your name used to welcome you is pleasant and highly appreciated.

5. **Showing respect.** It is important to be respectful of another person's point of view and to give them time to express it during social interactions. Even if you disagree with them, everyone has the right to express themselves. You may then express your stance when they have had a chance to do so.

6. **Being cooperative.** When working on a project, attempting to solve a job problem, or resolving an interpersonal issue,

cooperation is crucial. Being stubborn or rebellious makes things harder and the situation unproductive. When there is collaboration, cooperation, and reciprocity, all endeavours succeed.

7. **Being empathetic.** Empathy is the ability to put oneself in another's shoes. Empathy fosters trust and rapport with others, which enhances the connection. Empathy also helps people recognize that they are not alone and that life may be difficult at times for all of us.

8. **Smiling and being yourself.** Although it may seem easy simply smile and be yourself, many individuals feel the need to act and impress others when they meet them. They feel it is vital to create a good impression and end up seeming artificial and dishonest. When you smile and be yourself, you put people at ease and enable the natural flow of conversation to occur.

9. **Having a positive, optimistic attitude**. We are all naturally attracted to those who are upbeat and enthusiastic. People who are upbeat help us feel better about ourselves. We may be positive in every social engagement by approaching it with an open mind, being prepared to consider all sides of an issue, and being helpful. We are cheerful

and hopeful when we connect with people in a helpful, problem-solving manner.
10. **Inclusiveness.** Engaging and involving people in a discussion, endeavour, or exchange is an essential aptitude and leadership trait. When everyone contributes to a project, everyone benefits. Ideas flow, brainstorming occurs, and viable solutions emerge.

Chapter 5.3: Effective Communication: Improving your Social Skills

Building positive connections with others may significantly decrease stress and anxiety in your life. Indeed, increasing your social support is connected to overall improved mental health, since having strong friends may function as a "buffer" for emotions of worry and depression. This is particularly true if you are socially nervous and want to make friends but are either afraid to or unclear about how to approach them. You may even avoid social events as a consequence of these apprehensive sensations.

Unfortunately, one of the side effects of avoiding social interactions is that you never have the chance to:

- boost your self-esteem by connecting with others
- establish great communication skills to boost the likelihood of successful partnerships!

For example, if you are terrified of going to parties or asking someone out on a date, your lack of confidence and experience will make knowing how to handle these circumstances much MORE challenging (like what to wear, what to say, etc.). People often have essential talents but lack the courage to put them to use. In any case, practice will boost your confidence and enhance your communication abilities.

Importance of Communication Skill

Communication skills are essential for making (and keeping!) friends and creating a strong social support network. They also assist you in meeting your wants while being mindful of the needs of others. People are not born with strong communication abilities; they are developed via trial and error and continuous practice, just like any other talent!

You should practice the following communication skills:

- Nonverbal Communication
- Conversation Skills
- Assertiveness

Nonverbal Communication

Nonverbal communication accounts for a big portion of what we say to one another. What you communicate to others with your eyes or body language has the same impact as what you express with words. When you are worried, you may act in ways that are intended to keep you from connecting with others. You may, for example, avoid eye contact or talk very quietly. In other words, you are attempting to avoid communication to avoid being assessed poorly by others. Your body language and tone of voice, on the other hand, send important signals to people about you:

- Emotional state (e.g., impatience, fear)
- Attitude toward the audience (e.g., submissiveness, contempt)
- Knowledge of the topic

- Sincerity (do you have a hidden agenda?)

Thus, avoiding eye contact, standing far away from others, and speaking quietly communicate, "Stay away from me!" " or "Don't bother talking to me! " This is probably not the message you want to deliver. The actions listed below might help you get started in assessing and strengthening your nonverbal talents.

Step 1: Identifying Your Trouble Spots

To begin, ask yourself the following questions:

- Do I have trouble maintaining eye contact when talking with others?
- Do I smile too much because of nervousness? Too little?
- Do I slouch?
- Do I keep my head down?
- Do I speak with a timid voice?
- Do I talk too rapidly when I'm nervous?
- Do I cross my arms and legs?

You should be aware of the following nonverbal behaviours:

- Posture (e.g., head up and alert, leaning forward)
- Movement and gestures (e.g., keeping arms uncrossed)
- Physical distance (e.g., standing closer when talking to others)
- Make eye contact (e.g., making appropriate eye contact when talking)
- Facial expression (e.g., smiling warmly)
- The volume of Voice (speaking at a volume easily heard)
- The tone of Voice (e.g., speaking with a confident tone)

Step 2: Experiment with and practice nonverbal abilities.

- Try to practice just one skill at a time so that you can ensure mastery before moving on to the next.
- You might ask a trustworthy friend or family to provide feedback on your nonverbal conduct. This feedback may be beneficial

since we often do not realize how we seem to others.

- If you have the ability, record yourself having a discussion and take notice of what your body language may be indicating. Once you've identified a few potential problems, practice the right body language.

- You may also put your new nonverbal talents to the test in front of a mirror.

- Once you've developed some confidence and practised utilizing nonverbal communication abilities at home, put it to the test in real-life situations. Starting simple, such as chatting to shop clerks, tellers, and cashiers is a smart idea. Increase your eye contact while conversing with people, smile more, and pay attention to the emotions of others. Is the bank teller nicer or chattier if you make more eye contact and smile at her?

Conversation Skills

Starting and maintaining conversations is one of the most difficult obstacles for someone suffering from social anxiety. It is natural to struggle a little while making small chats since it is not always simple to think of things to say. This is especially true when you're worried! On the other hand, some worried peoples speak excessively, which may be off-putting to others.

Step 1: Identifying Your Trouble Spots

Here are some questions you may want to ask yourself to help you select the areas you wish to improve on:

- Do I have trouble starting conversations?
- Do I run out of things to say quickly?
- Do I say "yeah," nod, and attempt to keep other people talking to avoid having to speak?
- Am I reluctant to talk about myself?

Tips for Starting a Conversation:

- Begin a conversation by saying something general and non-personal, such as talking about the weather ("Gorgeous day, isn't it?"), paying a compliment ("That sweater looks great on you"), making an observation ("I noticed you were reading a sailing book, do you have a boat?"), or introducing yourself ("I don't think we've met, I'm...").

- You don't have to say anything particularly clever. It is preferable to be truthful and authentic.

- After a while, particularly if you've known the individual for a long, it could be okay to move on to more personal themes, such as relationships, family concerns, personal sentiments, spiritual views, and so on.

- Remember to be aware of your nonverbal behaviour - make eye contact and talk loudly enough for people to hear you!

Tips for Keeping a Conversation Going:

- Remember that a discussion is a two-way street; don't say too much or too little! When conversing one on one, strive to participate in around one-half of the discussion as much as feasible.

- Describe your weekend activities, favourite hockey team, or hobby or interest. Intimate information does not have to be "too personal"; you might begin by expressing your thoughts on movies and literature, or by discussing activities that you like.

- Try to be vulnerable: it's okay to confess that you're anxious (for example, "I never know what to say to break the ice," or "I'm always so worried at parties where I don't know anybody"). However, be cautious since exposing yourself too much too quickly might turn off others.

- Ask inquiries about the other person, but avoid asking too intimate questions while you are just getting to know someone. Appropriate inquiries may be about their weekend activities, preferences, or their thoughts on anything you mentioned. "How do you like that new restaurant?" for example.

- Ask open-ended inquiries rather than closed-ended ones. A closed-ended question can only be replied to with a few words, such as yes or no, such as "Do you enjoy your job?" An open-ended inquiry, on the other hand, evokes much more explanation; for example, "How did you get into your area of work?"

- Do I over-communicate when I'm nervous?

Remember: People often like talking about themselves, particularly when the other person is interested.

Tips for Ending a Conversation:

- Remember that all talks must come to an end at some point; don't feel rejected or nervous as the chat draws to a close! Running out of topics to discuss does not imply that you are a failure or that you are uninteresting.

- Consider a gentle method to conclude the discussion. For example, you may explain you need to refill your drink, meet up with someone at a party, or head back to work, or you could pledge to resume the discussion at a later time or date (for example, "Hope we'll get a chance to speak again" or "Let's have lunch again soon!").

Step 2: Experiment with and improve your conversation skills.

Try breaking some of your usual routines the next time you have the chance to practice beginning or concluding a conversation. For example, if you seldom talk about yourself, try sharing your ideas and emotions more often and watch what occurs. Alternatively, if you usually wait for the other person to terminate the discussion, consider making a gracious leave first.

Here are some ideas for some practice scenarios:

- **Speak to a stranger**: For instance, at a bus stop, an elevator, or while waiting in line.

- **Talk to your neighbours:** For example, you may talk about the weather or anything going on in your area.

- **Interact with co-workers**: Chat with coworkers, for example, during your coffee break or in the staffroom during lunch.

- **Have friends over for a get-together**: Invite a coworker or an acquaintance over, meet for coffee, or host a birthday celebration for a relative. Make an effort to communicate with your visitors!

- **Try giving a compliment:** Commit to offering at least two compliments every day, especially ones you would not ordinarily give. But remember to always be genuine: only offer someone praise if you believe what you're saying.

Chapter 5.4: Social and Communication Skills for Teen

How would you want to improve your connections with people in your home, with friends, and at school? Getting along with others seems vague and tough to achieve, so let's break it down into some more attainable and particular abilities. You will get along well with people if you develop the following skills:

- Building others' self-esteem.
- Showing empathy for others.
- Encourage individuals to collaborate.
- Communicating assertively.
- Asking productive questions and demonstrating listening skills.
- Responding productively to emotional statements.

People skills (also known as emotional intelligence) may be divided into six categories. Let's take a quick look at each of them.

Building others' self-esteem. You feel good when you are put in a scenario where you are made to feel good about yourself. You may do the same for others by engaging in the following activities:

- Make eye contact with others.
- Call others by their names.
- Ask others for their opinions.
- Compliment others' work.
- Tell people how much you appreciate them.
- Thank you letters should be written whenever someone accomplishes anything noteworthy.
- Make visitors to your house or office feel welcome.
- Take note of what is going on in other people's lives. Recognize significant life events and show worry about terrible life circumstances such as sickness, death, and accidents.
- When you encounter strangers in public, introduce your family members to them.
- Encourage those you care about to develop their skills and interests.

- Share your pals' joy when they achieve something.

- Honour people's needs and wants.

- Accept responsibility for your decisions and actions, and expect others to do the same.

- Take charge of the quality of your conversations.

Showing empathy for others. *Recognizing the feelings of another is what empathy entails.* It is the ability to put oneself in the shoes of another person and comprehend how he or she perceives reality and feels about things.

Being conscious of our emotions and how they influence our behaviour is a critical skill in today's environment, both at school and work. People who are emotionally disconnected are unable to connect with others. They seem to be emotionally tone-deaf. No one likes to be around such individuals since they are unaware of how their actions influence others. You've undoubtedly met a few folks that fit the bill.

Encouraging people to cooperate. There are certain particular things you can do while working or participating in activities with others in a group to assist establish an atmosphere where you will all function effectively together:

- Play no favourites. Everyone should be treated the same. Otherwise, some people will be sceptical of you.

- Don't gossip about others behind their backs.

- Request suggestions from others. Participation promotes dedication.

- Even if you are unable to carry out a request, follow up on recommendations, requests, and comments.

- When you make a declaration or an announcement, make sure everyone understands it. Don't presume that everyone is on your side.

- Ensure that individuals receive clear instructions for completing jobs. Inquire as to what individuals intend to accomplish.

- When they are cooperative, let them know you appreciate it. Take nothing for granted.

Communicating assertively. Assertive communication is a healthy approach to expressing one's views and ideas. People are not born forceful;

their conduct is the result of a mix of taught abilities. Assertiveness allows you to:

- Act in your own best interests
- Stand up for yourself without becoming anxious
- Express your honest feelings
- Assert your rights without rejecting others' rights.

Assertive conduct differs from passive or aggressive behaviour in the following ways:

- Self-expressive
- Honest
- Direct
- Sclf-cnhancing
- Constructive, not destructive

What you say and how you say it are both examples of assertive conduct.

Posing pertinent questions and displaying effective listening abilities. Listening skills allow you to demonstrate that you are hearing and comprehending what another person is saying and are interested in what he or she has to say.

Positively responding to emotive words. Active listening is a communication ability that is particularly beneficial in emotional circumstances because it allows you to convey that you comprehend what the other person is saying and how he or she feels about it. Active listening is repeating what the other person has stated in your own words. It's a test to see whether your comprehension is right. This shows that you are paying attention and are interested and concerned. Active listening replies consist of two parts:

- Identifying the emotion that the other person is expressing
- and stating the cause of the emotion

Here are some remarks on active listening:

- "Sounds like you're upset about what happened at school."
- "You're annoyed by my lateness, aren't you?"
- "You sound confused about how to solve this problem."
- "It makes you angry when you find errors in your homework."

- "It seems like you're quite concerned about Wendy."

- "I get the feeling you're busy right now."

Active listening is not synonymous with agreement. It is a means of indicating that you plan to listen to and comprehend another person's point of view.

The capacity to get along with others is a taught talent. Nobody is born knowing how to boost the self-esteem of others, demonstrate empathy, inspire collaboration, speak assertively, ask constructive questions, or react productively to emotional remarks. However, with enough work, these abilities may be learnt and improved. You will be able to form stronger connections at home and work if you take the time to acquire these abilities.

Chapter 5.5: Social Skills for Autistic Pre-Teens and Teenagers

Autistic teens' social skills include:

- Discovering what other individuals are thinking and feeling
- recognizing and interpreting facial expressions and body language adjusting to new social settings

- resolving social issues, such as what to do when you disagree with someone
- Recognizing unwritten societal rules
- Interests in common with other teens.

Social skills assist autistic teens in developing healthy interactions with classmates and making friends, which benefits their self-esteem, wellness, and feeling of belonging.

Whether your autistic kid has one or many friends or likes to be alone, social skills can help your child know how to respond in various social circumstances, such as chatting to a store clerk, participating in family events, or having fun at adolescent parties.

Social Skills Strategies for Autistic Teenagers

A variety of tactics may be used to assist autistic teens in developing their social skills. Some of these tactics may also be beneficial to teens who prefer to be alone but need to practice social skills for daily settings. Among the strategies are:

- role-play
- self-management techniques
- social groups
- social media

- social skills training
- social stories
- TV programs
- video-modelling
- visual supports

Role-play

You and your kid might practice skills like saying hello, asking for what you want, and saying thank you at a store. You might also attempt something connected to friendships, such as inviting a classmate to a weekend get-together.

You might ask your kid what skills and scenarios he or she would like to practice. Your youngster might also attempt acting out scenarios with other family members or friends.

Self-management techniques

If your autistic kid learns how to regulate their behaviour or what they need to do rather than depending on others to prod them, he or she will be able to acquire social skills. Your youngster might use tick sheets, stickers, or a wrist counter to keep track of how often they perform something. For example, if your kid is practising conversation skills, he or she may cross a sheet after each question they asked the other person.

Social groups

Your kid may choose to participate in a local social and recreational activity or organization to meet other autistic teens, exchange experiences, and make new friends. These clubs may be an excellent place for autistic teens to practice social skills and learn about social norms. Your state's autism service may direct you to local support groups.

Your youngster might potentially join a club or organization based on a hobby or unique interest. Because it provides your kid with something to speak about, this might make socialization simpler, to begin with.

Social media

Social networking may assist autistic teens in connecting with peers from school or activity groups. It allows them to take their time and consider what they want to say. It also eliminates the need to interpret nonverbal signals from others.

Social skills training

Some autism treatments and supports are intended to educate and strengthen social skills. Stop Think Do, for example, employs problem-solving techniques. The Secret Agent Society (SAS) is a program that may be obtained in the form of a computer game, a board game, or group therapy sessions. The Program for the Education and Enrichment of Relational Skills (PEERS®) teaches students how to create and maintain friendships.

Social stories

Social tales may help to explain social norms. A social tale, for example, may be used to describe what a social kiss is and when it is acceptable.

Social tales may also help your youngster consider things from the perspective of someone else. You may, for example, make up a tale about how your kid would feel if they are unable to do something they like, or how a friend could feel in the same scenario.

TV programs

Watching TV shows may provide your youngster with some suggestions about how to behave and not act in certain social settings. You may record a TV program episode and stop it to discuss what your kid would do next in that circumstance.

Video-modelling

To assist your youngster to develop social skills, you may purchase ready-made films or create your own.

You could, for example, film:

- Two of your pals engage in a prepared discussion that demonstrates how to start a conversation and what to say.
- your youngster taking turns, allowing your child to see themselves modelling the behaviour
- You may stop the movie and discuss nonverbal communication with your kid by observing people's facial expressions, body language, tone of speech, and so on.

Visual supports

Images may teach your autistic kid what to look for in various social settings. For example, you might use images to demonstrate how individuals indicate their want to engage in discussion. Someone may be staring at you and smiling, or they may be looking away and yawning. You might utilize photographs of people with various facial expressions and body language.

Prompt cards help your autistic kid remember what to do in various scenarios. For example, you may practice taking turns in a discussion by passing a 'My turn' card back and forth. Alternatively, your youngster might carry a cue card with instructions on how to begin and terminate a discussion.

Chapter 06: Essential Intellectual Skills

Chapter 6.1: Critical Thinking Skills

The critical thinking skills are:

- Analytical
- Communication

- Creativity
- Open-Minded
- Problem Solving

We are aware that the list is not entirely clear. That is why we wish to categorize these critical thinking abilities as "subskills." It will help you understand what "critical thinking abilities" are. Analytical Capabilities

Every young adult must carefully examine every piece of information he receives. If you don't comprehend the facts, there's a good risk you'll draw incorrect conclusions. Here are a few examples of critical thinking skills:

1. Data Analysis
2. Information Seeking
3. Asking "valuable" questions
4. Judgment
5. Recognizing differences and similarities, etc.

Communication

Children (and adults) often do not grasp what it means to have good communication skills. Verbal, nonverbal, and written communication are all examples of critical thinking abilities. It is only through improving each of your critical thinking abilities that you will be able to develop them properly. You mustn't miss any of them.

Here are a few examples of communication abilities:

1. Explanation
2. Collaboration
3. Presentation
4. Teamwork
5. Written communication (networking for example)
6. Interpersonal skills, etc.

Creativity

Creativity is always required for critical thinking abilities. Keep in mind that you may not be able to discover some pieces of information right away. That is why, from time to time, you must make predictions and picture what may happen if you make a choice. Here are some examples of creativity:

1. Curiosity

2. Imagination

3. Predicting

4. Synthesizing

5. Conceptualization, etc.

Open-Minded

Being objective is a difficult endeavour. However, every young adult will have the chance to discover that. It is impossible to develop critical thinking abilities if your mind is closed to it. If your mind is "closed," you will be unable to properly process the information you receive. Being open-minded requires you to be:

1. Inclusive

2. Fair

3. Observation

4. Reflection

5. Humble

Problem Solving

Fear of uncertainty is one of the primary reasons why young folks do not want to become entrepreneurs. It is difficult for them to deal with stress and ordinary concerns. That is why problem-solving is another critical thinking skill that students must develop.

Overcoming your worries and concentrating your efforts on the answer will teach you how to improve your critical thinking abilities. Here are some things you should have and work on:

1. Attention to details
2. Clarification
3. Decision-making
4. Innovative
5. Applying standards, etc.

Now that you understand what critical thinking abilities are, it is time to look at how to improve critical thinking skills. The process takes time and patience, so don't expect to have flawless critical thinking abilities by tomorrow.

How to Develop Critical Thinking Skills

Various stages will demonstrate how to build critical thinking abilities. To be more specific, there are eight stages you must do to attain your goal:

Let's look at ways to build critical thinking abilities together. We will add to this list with further explanations.

- **Ask Questions That Matter**

You already understand how vital it is to enrich oneself with useful knowledge. Those bits of knowledge, however, will not suddenly appear. You must seek them out. Still, the questions you ask must be excellent. Asking and investigating incorrect questions is a waste of time.

Finding accurate and relevant information is necessary for developing critical thinking abilities. Many children have easy access to a wealth of knowledge. But, can every piece of information you get to assist students to strengthen their critical thinking skills?

The Internet is a wonderful tool for locating the information you need. There are several blogs, vlogs, e-books, and other educational products available to assist you in becoming a better entrepreneur. These are the venues where knowledgeable, educated, and successful individuals discuss their personal and professional experiences.

- **Evaluate What You Hear**

Return to the section where we asked, "What are critical thinking skills?" ". An adolescent must examine all he hears. The information you get is not always accurate. Consider the following scenario: you wish to become the owner of an IT startup. It's no secret that you lack real-world and industrial experience. Eventually, you'll start asking inquiries about the company. However, this does not imply that you must agree with everything you hear.

Make a list of the recommendations you get. Read them attentively and consider what might happen if you followed the advice of others. This is the time to put your critical thinking abilities to work. Everything should be evaluated and thought about! Use your imagination to see the precise outcome of your choice or conclusion.

You will not allow someone to rule your life in this manner. You may make errors at first, but don't let them deter you. Remember that your errors are the finest teachers you can obtain. Furthermore, even the most successful businesses make errors.

- **Detect Sources of Information**

We've previously shown that not every viewpoint or conclusion we acquire is valid. However, the quality of information you get is heavily dependent on the source.

This information might have originated from a variety of sources. We may, for example, seek counsel from our parents, family members, and friends. It may also take the shape of an essay, book, film, podcast, or another medium. But, before you start listening, you need to figure out who is giving you the advice. When it comes to qualifying this knowledge, your critical thinking abilities will come in help.

Let us suppose you wish to locate a mentor. The majority of young individuals have no idea how to spot a good one. They believe that the most important feature to seek is years of expertise. However, it is unimportant in terms of your critical thinking abilities.

A great mentor combines expertise, life experience, and a desire to assist others in bettering their lives. To assist you, he must first comprehend your situation and sentiments. That is why, if you want to improve your critical thinking abilities, you must first identify your source of knowledge.

- **Research, Research, Research**

Critical thinking skills development is heavily reliant on your work and devotion. We previously said that you should do research about a mentor and ask pertinent questions. But keep in mind that you may always do your research.

The term "research" appears three times in our subheadings for a purpose. You must always seek to expand your knowledge. That manner of thinking will assist you in improving your critical thinking abilities. You will also become a better person and entrepreneur as a result of this experience.

Students often do not devote time to research. They are hoping for information that will assist them in making sound judgments and reaching appropriate conclusions.

Keep in mind that information may be found everywhere around us. If you cannot attend high-quality universities, that does not imply you cannot educate yourself. Google and YouTube can provide you with more information than you can fathom. The only need is that you DESIRE to do so. This is the only approach to improve your critical thinking capabilities.

- **Ask Yourself – "Am I Right?"**

Some young people are unable to accept constructive criticism. When someone tells them what to do or how to do things right, they get angered. Someone who has the authority to chastise them, such as their parents, instructors, or mentors. They believe they are under assault.

Objectiveness is one of the critical thinking skills that every adolescent must have. Being objective will not only boost your critical thinking abilities. It will also alter your outlook and way of living.

Young adults are not required to agree to everything they are taught. However, individuals must understand how to determine whether or not the advice is valuable to them. This is when critical thinking abilities come into play. They must be analytical and open-minded, among other qualities.

If a youngster wants to be an entrepreneur, they must realize that they will get both good and negative criticism along their company journey. But bear in mind that if the counsel comes from a genuine source, someone who actually loves and wishes you well, you should think about it.

Never lose sight of the fact that you are still young. Life will teach you many things in the future, but for now, you are still a youngster who has to grow up. Be impartial in all situations and should not attempt to dodge receiving comments on your job. This also implies that you must think for yourself. Making your conclusions and listening to others' comments are both parts of developing critical thinking abilities.

- **Improve Your Weaknesses / Strengthen Yourselves**

Some children believe that they are inferior to their peers. They are unclear about what to do and sometimes feel worthless. However, we all have unique skills. Some of them are just concealed deep inside our souls and need to be identified.

Take out a piece of paper. List what you do very well or where you excel in one column. Write down everything you need to work on in another column. Having a good understanding of your strengths and shortcomings allows you to make more informed decisions about your future path. Now, in a third column, list the things you plan to do to better yourself.

Do not put off your progress. Begin at the same time you place your pencil on the table. Remember that problem-solving is one of the critical thinking abilities. You have no choice except to SOLVE

YOUR PROBLEM. Remember that if these behaviours are properly addressed, they will have a significant impact on your achievement.

- **Keep it Simple**

Some may argue that "this is easier said than done." But don't worry, it's not as tough as you think. Developing your critical thinking abilities may be a rewarding and exciting journey. When children are required to accomplish something entirely new, they often experience stress. The adults are experiencing the same issue. So it makes no difference how old you are.

Do not be concerned if your critical thinking abilities stay stable over an extended length of time. This is a lengthy process, and becoming a better version of yourself takes time. Don't worry about running out of time. We hope you recognize that critical thinking skills development is a lifelong process. So, relish every minute of your progress and remember the Chapters you learned on that journey.

- **Repeat the Process**

It is not unexpected if a youngster becomes stuck at some time throughout the developmental stage. You cannot omit any of the above-mentioned steps since the repercussions would be disastrous. If anything similar occurs to you, go through the whole procedure again.

Reconsider your options. Remember that there is no time limit for self-improvement. As previously said, becoming a better version of oneself is a lifelong journey. Set reasonable deadlines. Maintain your motivation. And never lose faith in your ability to go ahead.

Conclusion: Benefits of Critical Thinking Skills Improvement

Now that you understand "what are critical thinking skills?" and "how to build critical thinking skills?" it is time to explore what you can gain out of them. We would like to emphasize the following advantages:

- Development of knowledge after school
- Making hard decisions
- Others won't manipulate you
- Becoming a successful entrepreneur

- Being independent!!!

Chapter 6.2: Organization Skills
Why Organization Skills Are Important

There are several reasons why we want our teenagers to be well-organized. The advantages of the organization have been shown in several studies. When things are disorderly, we experience more distraction and tension. Students who lack organizational abilities have greater academic obstacles, get poorer marks, and interact negatively with instructors. Many teenagers and young adults with special learning difficulties need specific instruction in organizational skills via tailored treatments. Even little gains in organizational abilities may reduce symptoms of inattention and enhance academic performance.

Organization And Other Executive Functioning Skills

It might be difficult to distinguish between your teen's or young adult's organizational challenges and other executive functioning abilities such as planning and time management. If your kid learns to utilize an organizing tool like a day planner, you're most likely also teaching them time management, prioritising, and planning skills.

Working memory and self-monitoring abilities will be required if your youngster learns to rearrange closets and preserve a neat area. That is why it is critical to detect and develop SMART objectives when teaching these skills—targeting certain habits may result in advantages in other areas.

Important Organization Skills for Teen
1. The Difference Between Neat and Messy

When we initially begin working on organization skills, one of the first questions we ask and assess is if the kid understands the difference between a clean, orderly room and a cluttered one. It may seem straightforward, but some people with special learning challenges may not analyze their surroundings in the same way you do.

Begin by searching for photographs online and asking your youngster to identify settings that seem clean and orderly. Show some photographs of abnormally dirty rooms, others that are crowded yet orderly, and some that may need some cleaning. Then move on to other areas of your home—you may even need to create some messes of your own!)

Can your youngster recognize and differentiate between the differences? If you don't, you're unlikely to be able to agree on what it means to be structured until you do. Continue to work on developing meaningful definitions of what it means to be organized so that both you and your adolescent can understand.

2. How to Use Designated Places

Ben Franklin is commonly quoted as stating, "A place for everything, and everything in its place." Work with your adolescent to establish a location for imported goods. Begin with a single category, such as "school materials" or "morning routine," then determine where each item goes. Use a label maker to indicate the proper location for objects if your adolescent benefits from visual suggestions. Take photographs of how a place appears after everything is put away, and then save them to your teen's phone or tablet in an album. They may utilize the picture book to get everything back in its proper location when they need to know where something is (or where to put things back when completed).

3. How to Start with A Clean Space

Decades of studies on organization and productivity have repeatedly shown that our brains operate better in clean, uncluttered environments. Teach your adolescent to begin each work session by cleaning up their workstation for a few minutes. Keep vital learning materials nearby and distractions out of sight. If your adolescent does not have a specific workstation in your house, collaborate to establish a clean and tidy environment that integrates your teen's furniture, décor, and location preferences. The more appealing it is for them to spend time in the surroundings, the more committed they will be to maintaining it clean and tidy.

4. How to Prep the Night Before

We've previously discussed the importance of using checklists and daily agendas to stay organized and on track, particularly as the day comes to a close. While we may expect our adolescents to 'just know' how to arrange for the following day's activities on their own, a more practical approach may be to employ an end-of-the-day reminder list. Teach your adolescent to prepare all of the tools and supplies they will need for the next day or the night before. They will not only develop a habit of organizing, but they will also be more likely to apply time management and self-management abilities to carry out the plan they have devised.

5. How to Use a Weekly Organization Checklist

Some of the leading gurus in organizing and planning advise followers to arrange tiny "tidy up" sessions rather than everything at once, which may rapidly become a gigantic effort. Teach your adolescent or young adult to perform a few different organizational activities every day to prevent having a big backlog of things to complete.

Begin by writing out all of the organizing and cleaning duties for the week. Put a * next to any jobs that must be accomplished daily rather than once a week. Then, split the duties equally across the seven days of the week. Allow your youngster to choose when they want to do certain duties. Keep the checklist in a visible place and praise your youngster for completing the activities as indicated.

6. The OHIO Rule

In addition to teaching your adolescent how to utilize a weekly organizing checklist, you should educate them on how to arrange and prioritize the chores they accomplish. For years, process engineers and organizational gurus have emphasized the OHIO Rule, or "Only Handle It Once," for chores such as email, paperwork, and homework.

You're providing your kid with a strong tool to enhance success by training them to begin and finish things as soon as they meet them, rather than putting them aside or returning to the same chores several times.

7. How to Recognize Overwhelm & Overload

Even if you use several of the tactics listed above, your adolescent will struggle with the organization at times. It occurs to everyone. What's more crucial is that you educate your adolescent on how to detect when their organizational techniques have failed, when they've strayed from utilizing the tools that encourage success, and when they're overburdened.

When stress and overload set in for many teenagers and young adults with special learning difficulties, they may resort to behavioural behaviours rather than conveying their need for assistance. Teaching your kid to notice these indicators and what to do at the time to halt and reset the organizing system will save everyone a lot of time and frustration.

Chapter 6.3: Adaptive Skills in Childhood

Adaptive skills in childhood are a collection of abilities required for everyday living. Maturity is influenced by adaptive abilities. They influence how a kid behaves in the household and community in terms of independence, personal responsibility, and making age-appropriate decisions.

These everyday life responsibilities are necessary for youngsters to evolve into adults and become self-sufficient members of society.

Adaptive skills are sometimes known as 'Activities of Daily Living,' or ADLs. Bathing, dressing, cleaning up, toilet training, and maintaining basic hygiene are some examples. Adaptive abilities in older teenagers and adults include navigating about town, making appointments, and being on time for a job or school.

Some youngsters might not seem to develop as rapidly as others. They seem to need extra assistance, instruction, and hand-holding to execute their daily responsibilities. Children with adaptive skills difficulties may have unique requirements. ASD, an intellectual impairment, or developmental disabilities are examples of exceptional needs. Very brilliant youngsters may have adaptive skills that may not match their abilities.

These adaptive abilities may be required in your exceptionally brilliant youngster who is reading two grade levels ahead. You may not be concerned about your child's learning. But you worry whether they'll ever get to school on time, bathe, or dress appropriately for the weather without your assistance.

You may have an 8-year-old kid, but you're already worried, "How can this child ever make it in college?" Children with ADHD or autism spectrum disorder (ASD) may have high intellect but poor adaptive abilities.

It's also worth noting that youngsters develop at various rates. Girls are said to develop more quickly than boys. We must alter our expectations for preterm newborns in very young children (up to the age of two or three) by taking gestational age at birth into account.

Symptoms of Adaptive Skill Issues in Children

- **Acts immature:** Not behaving as maturely as peers their age. Perhaps you're continually apologizing for inappropriate conduct at the grocery store, library, or playground.

- **Delayed developmental milestones:** At well-child checkups, your physician will inquire about your child's ability to talk, walk, dress, and bathe.

- **Cannot follow the morning routine:** Having difficulty getting dressed, eating, and cleaning your teeth without the assistance of others

- **Leaves clothes, toys, and belongings everywhere:** Feeling like a storm struck your living room once your kid arrives?

- **Needs help to bathe:** Still needs assistance in the shower, which is unusual for their age.

- **Resists hygiene and wears the same clothes:** If you don't step in to help, I'll be going to school with unclean, uncombed hair, unbrushed teeth, and the same clothing as yesterday.

- **Cannot manage daily skills:** Trouble telling time, reading a calendar, or calculating money; requires extensive assistance with everyday duties.

- **Does not do chores:** They are not putting their things away, taking out their garbage, or tidying their room.

Causes of Adaptive Skill Issues in Children

- **Immaturity:** Children who do not mature as quickly as their classmates will be more dependent on adult care and direction. There is some age variance, and genetics and environment may also play a role.

- **Lack of opportunity or responsibility given:** Some children may not live in a safe environment that allows them to be independent. Some families may provide refuge and care for their children so often that they struggle to acquire independence. Children will learn these abilities more slowly if they do not have the opportunity to attempt to dress, wash their teeth, or feed themselves.

- **Developmental delays:** Children who suffer developmental delays are more likely to have adaptive skill impairments as a result of this delay. It is important to use early intervention programs when they are available.

- **Cognitive impairment:** Children with cognitive delays or impairment (intellectual disability) often have equivalent delays in these behaviours and abilities.

- **Attention deficit hyperactivity disorder:** It is usual for children with ADHD to have weaker adaptive skills than cognitive ability. The development of adaptive skills is influenced by hyperactivity, impulsivity, and inattention.

- **Autism spectrum disorder:** Furthermore, children with autism have lesser adaptive skills than their cognitive capacities. Children may depend more on their parents or seem less mature than their classmates of the same age. They are having difficulty with social connections and communication.

- **Depression or mood challenges:** When a kid or adolescent is sad or experiencing mood difficulties, parents may notice a decrease in adaptive abilities. When coping with emotional weight, the child's cleanliness, maturity, and independence may suffer.

- **Motor coordination challenges:** Children with motor impairments, such as Developmental Coordination Disorder or Cerebral Palsy, may struggle to complete activities independently.

What to Do About Children's Adaptive Skills Issues

- **DO:** Break down abilities into basic stages and assist your child's development of these talents. Adapt tasks so that your youngster may learn them in little steps.

- **DO:** Help them pick up toys in the bedroom or rake the yard.

- **DO:** Make a morning routine poster to place in your child's bedroom and bathroom to remind them of the routines to follow.

- **DO:** Make a chore schedule with stickers that may be traded in for the family game night, ice cream, or a trip to the park. Maintain simplicity and make incentives meaningful.

- **Don't:** Threaten something you can't or won't enforce, like "No TV for a week if this room isn't tidy." If everyone else is watching TV, this outcome may not be conceivable.

- **DO:** "First, throw all of your dirty clothes in the hamper, then go outside," you say. This reward is instant and simple, and the task is described explicitly.

Chapter 6.4: Creative Thinking

Creative thinking is an important life ability since it allows us to create, develop, and adapt to unexpected or changing events. In light of the worldwide epidemic, we've all had to be creative in how we work, teach, and learn during the previous six months. We can see the value of promoting our pupils' creative thinking now more than ever.

When your children were tiny, there was seldom a need to promote creative play or original ideas - to small children, thinking outside the box is as natural as breathing and carries with it imaginative and artistic activities. As they reach adolescence, youngsters often grow self-conscious and hesitant of moving outside of their comfort zone. But all is not lost; it is never too late to inspire them!

1. Lead by Example

Leading by example is the greatest approach to fostering your teen's creativity. Perhaps you previously loved writing or dabbled in art, but it was buried behind the responsibilities of family life. Or maybe you attend your pottery class every week without fail. We all have a creative streak (even if it's buried deep under the surface or long forgotten), so whether you bake up a storm, have a flair for home furnishings, or a love for arithmetic (yeah, that counts, too), show it off to your adolescent.

2. It's Not Just About Arts & Crafts

Painting and writing are not the only forms of creativity. It's also about having inspired thoughts and being able to apply your creativity in daily situations. For example, if your kid is having difficulty with a certain portion of his or her schoolwork, try other approaches to get their creative juices flowing, such as brainstorming to come up with answers to their challenges, and motivating them to think outside the box. Use team-building activities as a family, or encourage your adolescents to collaborate on a task with friends or classmates, since constructively sharing views and ideas helps to promote creativity.

3. Encourage Questioning

Stimulate your adolescents to question everything they are unsure about and search for solutions to their questions as a great method to encourage creativity. Allow them to explore their ideas and views, and show them that not everyone feels the same way they do, which is OK. Show them that just because they have a different point of view than others does not make it incorrect, and assist your adolescent to realize that there is a way to express themselves strongly without being disrespectful or dismissive of others.

4. Don't Stifle Their Creativity

Encourage your teenagers to try something new, maybe an activity they haven't considered before, such as learning to play an instrument. Allow children to pick what they want to eat for supper, and encourage them to try something new. Try not to push your point of view too much, since even the most well-meaning parent may unintentionally restrict their teen's creativity by being too dictatorial. Back off if you find yourself dismissive or flippant about your teen's most outrageous notions or views, or if you are more concerned about the mess they are causing. An anxious, hovering parent is not favourable to creativity.

5. Let Them See It Is Okay to Take Risks

As children grow into teenagers, their willingness to take chances typically diminishes. They are much more aware of the often harsh environment around them, and attempting something new or partaking in an activity that is outside of their comfort zone might be frightening. It is critical to instil the notion that it is OK to fail at the first hurdle; that innovation may fail, but that this is acceptable. You will never succeed if you do not attempt.

6. Discover Life

Nature is the most amazing source of inspiration. Take your adolescent to the beach or on lengthy, meandering hikes through the woods. Encourage your children to take in their surroundings by stopping to enjoy a beautiful flower or nature's complex artwork on an aged tree trunk. Take in some fresh air and just enjoy the beauty that surrounds you.

Visit museums and galleries to immerse them in history, culture, and art. Take them to the ballet, a music event, or a fine-dining restaurant for supper. There's a huge world out there waiting to be discovered: a culturally aware kid, who has had the chance to experience variety, is much more receptive to being artistically inspired.

Chapter 6.5: Decision-Making/Problem-Solving with Teens

Every day, we make choices, large and little. Making decisions is a crucial ability to teach children of all ages because parents want their children to grow up to be self-sufficient, responsible, and joyful individuals. According to a certain study, individuals who can appraise a situation and make a choice are frequently more successful in life. Giving young children minor choices between two possibilities should help them develop decision-making abilities. As children grow into teenagers, they will need to learn to make more choices as they gain independence. Learning and using decision-making and the problem-solving process will assist teenagers in reaching this aim.

Teens must make an increasing number of choices that impact them. They will learn and develop from their accomplishments as well as their failures. If their parents make the majority of their choices for them, they will be unprepared to take on this responsibility as adults.

How can you, as a parent, assist them in developing decision-making skills? Teach them how to make choices and give them the authority to make them. You are often engaged in the process and may model suitable behaviours. This is also an excellent moment for you and your kid to establish communication.

Steps to Decision-Making/Problem Solving

1. Identify and define the problem.

Consider the best possible result or aim.

2. List possible options/alternatives.

Use a brainstorming approach in which you write down a lot of ideas. Allow the adolescent to come up with the initial concept and write it down, even if it doesn't seem feasible to her. If they are unable to begin (give them time to ponder first), ask if you may offer a proposal. Making it ridiculous may inspire kids to express themselves freely.

Continue until you can't think of any more ideas or choices. Remember to refrain from passing judgment. This is just a collection of ideas.

3. Evaluate the options.

Allow the kid to weigh his or her alternatives while you provide counsel, support, and encouragement. If you see an issue they aren't considering, ask them if you may bring it up. By requesting permission to bring up a topic, people are more likely to listen to your argument and not see it as a lecture or dismissal of their thoughts and thinking process.

The youngster may analyze their alternatives by asking the following questions: Is it cruel? Is it painful? Is it unjust? Is it deceptive? Is it in accord with the objective?

4. Choose one option.

The solution to the issue mustn't cause another problem.

5. Make a plan and do it.

This is most likely the most challenging stage. If their selection is not acceptable to the other person, they may need to return to the list of possibilities.

6. Evaluate the problem and solution.

This is perhaps the most overlooked decision-making stage, yet it is crucial to the learning process. Consider: What caused the problem? Can a similar issue be avoided in the future? How was the current issue resolved? They may be pleased with their accomplishments, or they can learn and accept responsibility for seeking another solution. If their plan does not work, avoid stating, "I told you so."

Cooperative Problem Solving

Parent-teen disputes may be resolved via cooperative problem-solving. It is based on the six-step decision-making process.

1. Present the problem.

2. Seek out agreements that result in solutions.

Parents should seek agreement at all times. Keep an eye out for the transition from "let's work this out" to "let's fight."

3. Collect information on everyone's perspectives.

For example: When you ask an adolescent to perform a task, he or she either refuses or becomes extremely upset with you. It is frequently preferable to wait until both of you are calm. Inquire with the adolescent about how he or she feels about completing chores. "It wasn't a nice time for me," the teenager may say.

4. Stick to the issue and listen.

Instead of responding sarcastically, "It never seems to be a good moment," consider echoing their feelings: "So you were busy at the time?" When children begin to express their emotions, parents must listen closely to the sentiments that lie underneath the words. They may not be accustomed to expressing their emotions and may be fearful of a lecture. "Yes, I detest it when you say 'Do it immediately,'" he or she would remark. Parent: "I had no clue you were feeling that way. Do you have any further thoughts about it?"

5. Keep asking: "Is there anything else?"

It's critical to keep asking this question until everything comes out. Otherwise, you'll most likely be dealing with surface problems rather than fundamental ones. To test whether you understand, use comments that mirror what they have just said: "Is it your least favourite task?" Then inquire, "Is there anything else?"

6. Reflect on your understanding.

Try to recap and repeat what your adolescent just stated to you in a calm, neutral manner. If your kid insists that's not what he or she meant, ask him or her to explain. By this time, the parent should be aware of how their adolescent feels about the topic, as well as how others feel about it.

7. Share your perceptions.

Sharing your perspectives with your children before asking whether they are eager to listen is one method to ensure a nonreceptive adolescent audience. Getting their approval first creates a beautiful atmosphere that encourages listening and collaboration. Share your perspectives on the situation when they have consented to listen. Maintain your cool and don't put them down. Simply express your emotions.

8. Request that your teen express their understanding.

Parent: "Could you just tell me what you just heard me say?" Allow them to reply. A parent might answer by saying that they were not condemning them, but were only expressing their emotions. Also, mention that you understand that it may be different for them, which is OK.

9. Brainstorm for solutions.

You've both spoken your opinions and emotions and had them respected by the other (validated). It's time to ask, "Can we see if we can come up with some ideas that we can both live with?" Then generate ideas.

- Agree on a solution.
- Set a date for evaluation.
- Follow through.

The responsibility of a parent is to educate their children. They learn respect by being courteous. They learn responsibility by following through on our promises and being accountable. We demonstrate by example. The classic adage, "Do as I say, not as I do," does not cut it and does not provide the intended result.

Teen brains are still being built. Parents must also recognize that, although this is an essential ability to teach and develop, teenagers are still more inclined to make rash judgments and act on impulse.

Chapter 6.6: Communication Skills

Without a question, we are living in a unique period in history. However, there is never a terrible moment to develop your communication skills.

Here are some helpful hints for your teenagers to enhance their talents.

1. Listen more, talk less.

People like to feel heard, so one method to enhance communication skills is to fully listen to what the other person is saying before formulating your answer. The person you are conversing with should be the most important in your life. To minimize misconceptions, ask for explanations and limit yourself to one discussion at a time. This implies that if you're on the phone with someone, don't react to an email or send a text at the same time.

2. Know your audience.

What you say depends on whom you're speaking with. Whether speaking with a buddy, it is OK to use casual language; but, when emailing or texting your manager, instructor, tutor, or supervisor, informal words such as "Hey" and "TTYL" have no place in your communication. You cannot presume that the other person understands the slang you use with your pals. If you want to enhance your communication abilities, remember to keep the other person in mind while conveying your message.

3. Body language matters.

This vital communication ability applies to both face-to-face and video conferencing. Open body language conveys the idea that you are approachable. Maintain eye contact and keep your arms uncrossed so the other person knows you're paying attention. When participating in video conferences, try to look at the camera rather than the screen. It makes a significant difference.

4. Check your messages before sending them.

Spelling and grammar checkers are not perfect. To enhance your communication abilities, double-check your writing to ensure that your words are conveying your intended meaning. Be succinct while conveying your desired message. After you've finished composing your message, take a break and return to it a few minutes later to review it. Before you press the send button, consider how you would respond if this were sent to you. When replying to an email, be sure to read the full content before answering.

5. Write things down.

Take notes as you would in a classroom if you want to enhance your communication abilities. When you're talking to someone else or at a meeting, don't depend on your recollection. Send a follow-up email to ensure that you understood everything mentioned during the chat. It doesn't have to be awkward—you may inform the person with whom you're conversing that taking notes is a habit that helps you keep organized. This is extremely useful while networking.

6. Picking up the phone is sometimes preferable.

If you have a lot to say, make a phone call rather than send a message. Email and direct messages on social media are good for various sorts of communication, but a two-way conversation allows for the natural ebb and flow.

7. Think before you speak.

Always pause before speaking, and treat everyone with respect. Take a time to think about what you're going to say and how you're going to say it. Teaching yourself to pause before responding can make you look mature and considerate to your audience.

8. Maintain a positive attitude and smile.

People will react positively to you if you smile and show a happy attitude. Even if you're on the phone, smiling and concentrating on portraying a positive disposition will alter how you communicate. This is a basic, sometimes forgotten behaviour that may have a significant influence on many of your talks.